Know SHIPS

Guide to Boatwatching on the Great Lakes and St. Lawrence Seaway, **1996**

37th Edition - Updated Annually

Copyright - 1996
ISBN No. 0-9636930-6-5

Marine Publishing Co., Inc.

Box 68, Sault Ste. Marie, MI 49783

E-mail: **rlkysbook@aol.com**

Founder: **Tom Manse, 1915-1994**

Roger LeLievre, Editor and Publisher

Researchers: *John Vournakis, Philip A. Clayton, Angela S. Clayton, Neil Schultheiss and Albert G. Ballert*

> **On the front cover:** The 1929-vintage self-unloader **Calcite II** sails past Fort Gratiot Light and into Lake Huron.

> **On the back cover:** The museum ship **Valley Camp** at Sault Ste. Marie, Michigan. See Page 112 for details.

CONTENTS

Lon W. Morgan

E.M. Ford, built in 1898, is the oldest operating vessel on the lakes.

The information in this book was obtained from the United States Coast Pilot (Vol. 6), the St. Lawrence Seaway Authority, the Lake Carriers Association, Farwell's Rules of the Nautical Road, the Institute for Great Lakes Research, the Great Lakes Commission, Jane's Merchant Ships, the American Merchant Seaman's Manual, the U.S. Army Corps of Engineers and other sources.

1,000-footer Walter J. McCarthy Jr., upbound at Detroit.   Richard I. Weiss

The GREAT LAKES AREA ...

... bounded generally on the north by Canada and on the south by the United States, is home to one of the greatest industrial complexes in the world. Steel plants here produce more than 30 percent of the world's steel, calling upon the iron, coal, petroleum and limestone resources of the continent. Agricultural areas produce vast grain harvests transported, in large measure, by way of the lakes in uniquely designed ships, during the 9-10 month navigation season.

The variety of general cargo that moves on the Great Lakes and St. Lawrence Seaway is diverse and considerable in volume. With an area of about 1,200,000 square miles/3,108,000 square kilometers (one-sixth of North America), the region produces about 78 percent of North America's steel and more than 40 percent of its food and feed.

To handle Great Lakes traffic there has evolved a special type of vessel, the North American "laker." These vary in size, the largest lakers being 1,000 feet/304.8 meters long, capable of carrying up to 60,000 tons/60,966 tonnes of iron ore or 1,700,000 bushels/45,552.5 tonnes of grain.

Many of the world's merchant ships also trade on the Great Lakes, entering via the St. Lawrence Seaway, which opened in 1959. The construction of large locks and the deepening of channels from Duluth to Montreal has helped bring ships of all nations to our doorsteps.

From the heartland of America to the heartland of the world, we dedicate this book!

GREAT LAKES LOADING PORTS

IRON ORE	LIMESTONE	COAL	GRAIN	CEMENT
Duluth	Port Inland	Superior	Thunder Bay	Charlevoix
Superior	Cedarville	Thunder Bay	Duluth	Alpena
Two Harbors	Drummond	Chicago	Milwaukee	**GYPSUM**
Taconite	Island	Toledo	Chicago	Port Gypsu
Harbor	Calcite	Sandusky	Saginaw	Alabaster
Marquette	Stoneport	Ashtabula	Sarnia	**PETROLE**
Escanaba	Marblehead	Conneaut	Toledo	East Chica
			Huron	Sarnia

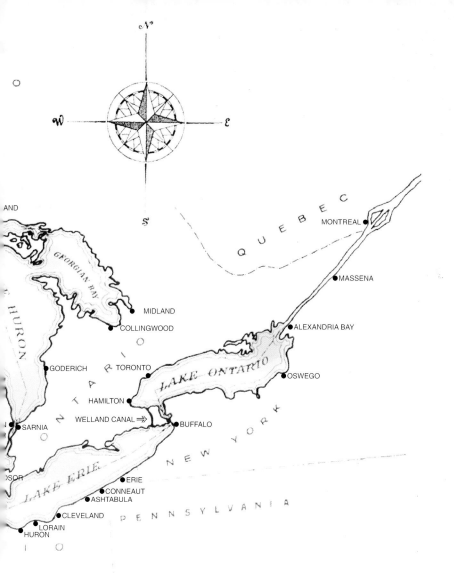

Unloading Ports

The primary iron ore and limestone receiving ports are Cleveland, Lorain, Chicago, Gary, Burns and Indiana harbors, Detroit, Toledo, Ashtabula and Conneaut. Coal is carried to Milwaukee, Green Bay and a host of smaller ports in the U.S. and Canada. Most grain loaded on the lakes is destined for export via the St. Lawrence Seaway. Cement is delivered to terminals stretching from Duluth to Buffalo. Tankers bring petroleum products to cities as diverse in size as Cleveland and Detroit or Escanaba and Muskegon.

The GREAT LAKES

Lake Superior

According to most references, the Seaway system begins at Duluth-Superior, at the western-most end of Lake Superior. Ore from the Minnesota iron ranges, grain, and low-sulfur 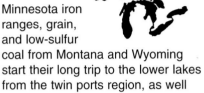 coal from Montana and Wyoming start their long trip to the lower lakes from the twin ports region, as well as from nearby Two Harbors, Taconite Harbor and Silver Bay. Iron ore is also shipped from the Marquette Range, while grain is exported from the Canadian lakehead at Thunder Bay. Lake Superior itself can boast of being the single largest body of freshwater in the world, measuring 383 miles (616.4 km) in length, 160 miles (257.5 km) at its widest point and 1,333 feet (406.3 m) at its deepest. Known for its fall fury, Lake Superior's November weather has claimed many sturdy ships and men.

Lake Michigan

The second-largest of the Great Lakes is 321 miles (516.6 km) long, 118 miles (189 km) wide and 932 feet (281.3 m) at its deepest. Vessels calling at Escanaba load taconite consigned to Chicago-area steel mills, while grain and manufactured goods ship to ports worldwide from Milwaukee, Green Bay and Chicago through the St. Lawrence Seaway.

Lake Huron

Lake Huron, at 247 miles (397.5 km) long, 183 miles (294.5 km) wide and 750 feet (228.6 m) at its deepest point, is fed from Lake Superior by the St. Mary's River. Collingwood, on Georgian Bay, has a rich shipbuilding history, while Goderich enjoys an active grain and salt trade. On the U.S. side, Calcite specializes in the shipment of limestone while Alpena is a major loading port for cement.

Lake Erie

The shallowest of the Great Lakes is 210 feet (64 m) at its deepest, 241 miles (387.8 km) long and 57 miles (91.7 km) wide. Ore and coal shipped to Toledo, Cleveland, Ashtabula, Conneaut, Erie and Buffalo feed the industrial appetites of the region, while the same ports are major trans-shipment points for cargos bound overseas. The Welland Canal connects lakes Erie and Ontario.

Lake Ontario

The most easterly of the Great Lakes is also the smallest, measuring 193 miles (310.6 km) in length and 53 miles (85.3 km) in width. The Canadian ports of Toronto and Hamilton enjoy brisk grain and ore trades, and play host to many saltwater vessels, while Ogdensburg, NY marks the start of the St. Lawrence River that runs eventually into the Atlantic Ocean.

Rod Burdick

Edgar B. Speer calls at Escanaba on 28 August, 1994.

ST. LAWRENCE SEAWAY

The St. Lawrence Seaway is a deep waterway extending some 2,300 miles (3,701.4 km) from the Atlantic Ocean to the head of the Great Lakes at Duluth, including Montreal harbor and the Welland Canal. More specifically, it is the system of locks and canals (both U.S. and Canadian), opened in 1959, that allow vessels to pass from Montreal to the Welland Canal at the western end of Lake Ontario. The vessel size limit within this system is 740 feet (225.6 meters) long, 78 feet (23.8 meters) wide and 26 feet (7.9 meters) draft.

Closest to the ocean is the **St. Lambert Lock,** which lifts ships some 15 feet (4.6 meters) from Montreal harbor to the level of the Laprairie Basin, through which the channel sweeps in a great arc 8.5 miles (13.7 km) long to the second lock. The **Cote St. Catherine Lock,** like the other six St. Lawrence Seaway locks, is built to the following standard dimensions:

Length 766 feet (233.5 meters)... Width 80 feet (24.4 meters)
Depth over sills 30 feet (9.1 meters)

The Cote St. Catherine requires 24 million gallons (90.9 million liters) to fill and can be filled or emptied in less than 10 minutes. It lifts ships from the level of the Laprairie Basin 30 feet (9.1 meters) to the level of Lake St. Louis, bypassing the Lachine Rapids. Beyond it, the channel runs 7.5 miles (12.1 km) before reaching Lake St. Louis.

The **Lower Beauharnois Lock,** bypassing the Beauharnois Power House, lifts ships 41 feet (12.5 meters) and sends them through a short canal to the **Upper Beauharnois Lock**, where they are again lifted 41 feet (12.5 meters) to reach the level of the Beauharnois Canal. After a 13 mile (20.9 km) trip in the canal, and a 30 mile (48.3 km) voyage through Lake St. Francis, vessels reach the U. S. border and the **Snell Lock,** which has a lift of 45 feet (13.7 meters) and empties into the 10-mile (16.1 km) long Wiley-Dondero Canal. After passing through Wiley-Dondero, ships are raised another 38 feet (11.6 meters) by the **Dwight D. Eisenhower Lock,** after which they enter Lake St. Lawrence, the pool upon which HEPCO and PASNY draw for water used in the power generating turbines a mile to the north.

At the Western end of Lake St. Lawrence, the **Iroquois Lock** allows ships to bypass the Iroquois Control Dam. The lift here is only about one foot (.3 meters). Once in the waters west of Iroquois, the ship channel meanders through the scenic Thousand Islands to Lake Ontario, the Welland Canal and eventually Lake Erie.

Welland Canal Locks 4, 5 and 6, at Thorold have a combined lift of 139.5 feet (42.5 meters).

LOCKS and CANALS

The Soo Locks
and St. Mary's River

Connecting Lake Superior with Lake Huron, the 80 mile (128.7 km) long St. Mary's River is a beautiful waterway that includes breathtaking scenery, picturesque islands and more than its share of hazardous twists and turns.

Remote Isle Parisienne marks its beginning; the equally-lonely DeTour Reef light marks its end. In between, are two marvels of engineering, the West Neebish Cut, a channel literally dynamited out of solid rock, and the Soo Canal, which stands where Native Americans in their dugouts once challenged the St. Mary's Rapids.

The first lock was built on the Canadian side of the river by the Northwest Fur Co. in 1797-98. That lock was 38 feet (11.6 meters) long and barely 9 feet (2.7 meters) wide. The first ship canal on the American side, known as the State Canal, was built from 1853-55 by engineer Charles T. Harvey. There were two tandem locks on masonry, each 350 feet (106.7 meters) long by 70 feet (21.3 meters) wide, with a lift of about 9 feet (2.7 meters).

The locks were destroyed in 1888 by excavators making way for the canals of the future.

Present Locks and Canals

MacArthur Lock

Named after Gen. Douglas MacArthur, the MacArthur Lock measures 800 feet (243.8 meters) long between inner gates, 80 feet (24.4 meters) wide and 31 feet (9.4 meters) deep over the sills. The lock was built by the United States in the war years 1942-43 and opened to traffic 11 July, 1943. The maximum sized vessel that can transit the MacArthur Lock is 730 feet (222.5 meters) long by 75 feet (22.9 meters) wide. In emergencies, this limit may be exceeded for vessels up to 767 feet (233.8 meters) in length.

Poe Lock

The Poe Lock is 1,200 feet (365.8 meters) long, 110 feet (33.5 meters) wide and has a depth over the sills of 32 feet (9.8 meters). Named after Col. Orlando M. Poe, it was built by the United States in the years 1961-68. The Poe Lock's vessel limit is 1,100 feet (335.3 meters) long by 105 feet (32 meters) wide and is the only lock now capable of handling vessels of that size. There are currently 30 vessels sailing the lakes restricted by size to the Poe Lock.

Davis Lock

Named after Col. Charles E.L.B. Davis, the Davis Lock measures 1,350 feet (411.5 meters) long between inner gates, 80 feet (24.4 meters) wide and 23 feet (7 meters) deep over the sills. It was built by the United States in the years 1908-14 and now sees only limited use due to its shallow depth.

Sabin Lock

Measuring the same as the Davis Lock, the Sabin Lock was built from 1913-19. Named after L.C. Sabin, the lock is currently inactive.

All traffic through the Soo Locks is passed toll-free.

The MacArthur Lock at Sault Ste. Marie, emptied for winter repairs.

As many as 600 different vessels pass through the Soo Locks yearly, varying in size from pleasure craft to large vessels carrying more than 60,000 tons (60,966 metric tons) of freight in a single cargo.

Vessels in the St. Mary's River system are under control of the U.S. Coast Guard at Sault Ste. Marie, and are required to check in with Soo Control on VHF Ch.12 (156.600 Mhz) at various locations in the river. In the vicinity of the locks, they fall under jurisdiction of the Lockmaster, who must be contacted on VHF Ch. 14 (156.700 Mhz) for transit reports, lock assignments and other instructions.

The Sault, ON Ship Canal

The present Canadian lock was constructed in 1887-95 through St. Mary's Island on the north side of the St. Mary's Rapids. It is the most westerly canal on the Seaway route. It was cut through red sandstone and is 7,294 feet (2,223.4 meters), or about 1.4 miles (2.2 km) long, from end to end of upper and lower piers.

The lock itself is 900 feet (274.3 meters) long, 60 feet (18.3 meters) wide and 21 feet (6.4 meters) deep. The approaches above and below the lock were dredged through boulder shoals. Failure of a lock wall in 1987 closed the canal, however preliminary repair work has begun that could see the waterway reopened for pleasure boaters by 1997.

Detroit River, Lake
St. Clair, St. Clair River

The Detroit River, from its mouth at Detroit River Light in Lake Erie

Cont'd on Page 12

Cont'd from Page 11

to Windmill Point Light at its head in Lake St. Clair, divides the United States and Canada for 32 miles (51.5 km).

Passing Bois Blanc Island, Grosse Ile and Grassy Island, the lower part of the river is divided into the Amherstburg Channel (for upbound vessels), the Livingstone Channel (for downbound) and the Trenton channel.

Lake St. Clair, measuring 26 miles (41.8 km) long and only 21 feet (6.4 meters) deep, is popular with pleasure boaters, but is especially violent during thunderstorms and fall gales.

The St. Clair River, about 39 miles (62.8 km) long from its mouth at Lake St. Clair to its head at Port Huron, is among the busiest waterways in the world. The river's lower third is a vast delta through which numerous channels empty into Lake St. Clair, while the upper two thirds consists of a single, deep channel. At the upper end of the river are Port Huron, Sarnia and the Blue Water Bridge.

The Welland Canal

The 27-mile long (43,5 km) Welland Canal overcomes a difference in water level of 326 feet (99.4 meters) between lakes Erie and Ontario. Locks 1-7 of the canal are lift locks, while Lock 8 (at 1,380 feet (420.6 km) the longest lock in the world) is a guard lock. Locks 4, 5 and 6 are twinned and placed end to end, looking like giant stair-steps. All locks (except Lock 8) are 829 feet (261.8 meters) in length, 80 feet (24.4 meters) wide and 30 feet (9.1 meters) deep. The maximum sized vessel that may transit the canal is 740 feet (225.6 meters) in length, 78 feet (24.4 meters) wide and 26 feet (7.9 meters) of draft. Connecting channels are kept at a minimum of 27 feet (8.2 meters), allowing vessels drawing 26 feet (7.9 meters) fresh water draft to transit the canal.

Lock 1 is at Port Weller, 2 is between there and Homer, 3 is south of Homer. At Thorold, the twinned locks 4, 5 and 6, are controlled with an elaborate interlocking system for safety. The flight locks have an aggregate lift of 139.5 feet (42.5 meters) and are similar to the Gatun locks on the Panama Canal. Just south of the flight locks is Lock 7, giving the final lift up to Lake Erie. The guard lock at Port Colborne completes the process.

All vessel traffic though the canal is regulated by a traffic control center. Upbound vessels must contact Seaway Welland off Port Weller on VHF Ch. 14 (156.700 Mhz), while downbound vessels must make contact off Port Colborne.

Vessels transiting the St. Lawrence Seaway must pay tolls based on registered tonnage and cargo on-board.

HOW A LOCK OPERATES

This trio of diagrams show how a vessel is lowered in a lock - a ship is raised by reversing the operation. No pumps are used; the water is merely allowed to seek its own level.

1. With both upper and lower gates **closed,** with the emptying valve **closed** and the filling valve **open,** the lock chamber is filled to the upper level. The upper gates are opened, allowing the ship to enter the chamber.

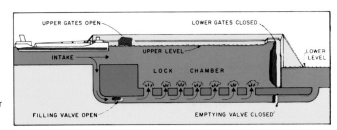

2. The ship is in the lock chamber. The upper gates and the filling valves are **closed.** The emptying valve is **opened** to allow water to flow from the lock to the lower level.

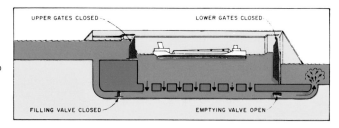

3. Once the water level in the lock chamber is at the lower level, the lower gates are **opened,** and the ship leaves the lock.
Now the lock is ready for an upbound vessel to be lifted to the higher level, or the lock may be refilled to lower another downbound ship.

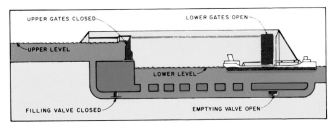

Courtesy U.S. Army Corps of Engineers

Pumps may be used after the close of navigation to remove water from the lock. Considerable maintenance is done during the winter, when the waterway is closed and most vessels are in lay-up.

MILEAGE BETWEEN PORTS

Left portion is miles, right portion is kilometers.

(In the table below: lower-left triangle values are **miles**; upper-right triangle values are **kilometers**. Abbreviations — TB = Thunder Bay, Dul = Duluth, Mar = Marquette, SSM = Sault Ste. Marie, Esc = Escanaba, Mil = Milwaukee, Chi = Chicago, Gar = Gary, Alp = Alpena, Col = Collingwood, PH = Port Huron, Det = Detroit, Tol = Toledo, Cle = Cleveland, Con = Conneaut, Buf = Buffalo, PC = Port Colborne, Tor = Toronto, Kin = Kingston, Mon = Montreal.)

	TB	Dul	Mar	SSM	Esc	Mil	Chi	Gar	Alp	Col	PH	Det	Tol	Cle	Con	Buf	PC	Tor	Kin	Mon
Thunder Bay	—	313.8	275.2	439.3	791.8	999.4	1104.0	1124.9	659.8	854.5	872.2	972.0	1058.9	1144.2	1235.9	1390.4	1364.7	1453.2	1664.0	1950.5
Duluth	195	—	420.0	634.1	988.1	1195.7	1300.3	1319.6	856.1	889.9	1068.6	1168.3	1256.9	1340.5	1432.3	1506.3	1561.0	1649.5	1860.4	2146.8
Marquette	171	261	—	255.9	608.3	817.5	922.1	941.4	478.0	672.7	690.4	790.1	877.1	962.4	1054.1	1208.6	1182.8	1271.3	1482.2	1768.6
Sault Ste. Marie	273	394	159	—	352.4	561.6	666.3	685.6	220.5	416.8	432.9	532.7	619.6	704.9	796.6	952.7	925.3	1014.0	1224.7	1511.1
Escanaba	492	614	378	219	—	323.5	440.9	463.5	392.7	605.1	605.1	704.9	791.8	877.1	968.8	1124.9	1097.5	1186.1	1396.9	1663.3
Milwaukee	621	743	508	349	201	—	136.8	165.8	601.9	812.7	814.3	914.1	1001.0	1086.3	1178.0	1332.5	1306.8	1395.3	1606.1	1892.5
Chicago	686	808	573	414	274	85	—	40.2	706.5	917.3	918.9	1018.7	1107.2	1190.9	1282.6	1437.1	1411.4	1499.9	1710.7	1997.1
Gary	699	820	585	426	288	103	25	—	725.8	936.6	938.2	1038.0	1124.9	1210.2	1301.9	1456.4	1430.7	1519.2	1730.0	2016.5
Alpena	410	532	297	137	244	374	439	451	—	297.7	252.7	352.4	439.3	524.6	616.4	770.9	754.1	833.6	1044.4	1330.9
Collingwood	531	553	418	259	376	505	570	582	185	—	415.2	515.1	601.9	687.2	778.9	933.4	907.6	996.2	1207.0	1493.4
Port Huron	542	664	429	269	376	506	571	583	157	258	—	99.8	186.7	273.6	363.7	518.2	492.4	581.0	791.8	1078.2
Detroit	604	726	491	331	438	568	633	645	219	320	62	—	86.9	173.8	263.9	420.0	392.7	481.2	692.0	978.5
Toledo	658	781	545	385	492	622	688	699	273	374	116	54	—	154.5	252.7	408.8	381.4	469.9	680.7	967.2
Cleveland	711	833	598	438	545	675	740	752	326	427	170	108	96	—	115.9	283.2	257.5	346.0	556.8	843.3
Conneaut	768	890	655	495	602	732	797	809	383	484	226	164	157	72	—	172.2	148.1	236.6	447.4	733.8
Buffalo	864	936	751	592	699	828	893	905	479	580	322	261	254	176	107	—	35.4	123.9	334.7	621.2
Port Colborne	848	970	735	575	682	812	877	889	463	564	306	244	237	160	92	22	—	88.5	299.3	585.8
Toronto	903	1025	790	630	737	867	932	944	518	619	361	299	292	215	147	77	55	—	259.1	543.9
Kingston	1034	1156	921	761	868	998	1063	1075	649	750	492	430	423	346	278	208	186	161	—	292.9
Montreal	1212	1334	1099	939	1046	1176	1241	1253	827	928	670	608	601	524	456	386	364	338	182	—

LEFT PORTION IS MILES, RIGHT PORTION IS KILOMETERS

MEANINGS OF BOAT WHISTLES

1 SHORT: *I am directing my course to starboard (right) for a port to port passing.*

2 SHORT: *I am directing my course to port (left) for a starboard to starboard passing.*

5 OR MORE SHORT BLASTS SOUNDED RAPIDLY: *Danger.*

1 PROLONGED: *Vessel leaving dock.*

3 SHORT: *Vessel moving astern.*

1 PROLONGED, SOUNDED ONCE PER MINUTE: *Vessel moving in fog.*

1 SHORT, 1 PROLONGED, 1 SHORT: *Vessel at anchor in fog.*

3 PROLONGED and 2 SHORT: *Salute.*

1 PROLONGED and 2 SHORT: *Master's salute.*

Some of these signals are listed in the pilot rules, while others have been adopted through common use.

Lakes Log

The **Cuyahoga** is the last vessel on the lakes powered by a Lentz Poppet quadruple expansion steam engine. The last two operating vessels powered by Skinner Uniflow steam engines are the carferry **Badger** and the cement carrier **Medusa Challenger**. The **Badger** is also the last coal-fired vessel on the lakes.

NAUTICAL MEASUREMENTS

Deadweight Tonnage: *the actual carrying capacity of a vessel, equal to the difference between the Light displacement tonnage and the Heavy displacement tonnage, expressed in long tons (2,240 pounds or 1,016.1 kg).*

Displacement Tonnage: *the actual weight of the entire vessel and everything aboard her, measured in long tons. The displacement is equal to the weight of the water displaced by the vessel. Displacement tonnage may be qualified as Light, indicating the weight of the vessel without cargo, fuels, stores or Heavy, indicating the weight of the vessel fully loaded with cargo, fuel and stores.*

Gross Tonnage: *the internal capacity of a vessel, measured in units of 100 cubic feet (2.83 cubic cubic meters) = a gross ton.*

Net Registered Tonnage: *the internal capacity of a vessel, measured in units of 200 cubic feet (2.83 cubic meters) but does not include the space occupied by boilers, engines, shaft alleys, chain lockers, officers and crew's quarters. Net registered tonnage is usually referred to as registered tonnage or net tonnage and is used to figure taxes, canal tolls and port charges.*

A knot: *one nautical mile per hour. The international nautical mile equals 6,076 feet (1,852 meters). A land mile is 5,280 feet (1,609.3 meters). Miles or kilometers are generally used on the Great Lakes for measurement.*

The GREAT LAKES SELF-UNLOADER

Once considered little more than an oddity, self-unloaders have evolved during the latter part of this century to become the preferred design for bulk ore, coal and stone carriers on the Great Lakes.

A self-unloader is just what its name implies - a vessel able to discharge its cargo using a system of conveyor belts and gates beneath the cargo holds and a movable boom, usually located on deck, that can be swung over either side of the ship. No dockside assistance is needed.

Self-unloaders first made an appearance in the 1920s, and became the mainstay of the coal, stone and cement trades shortly thereafter. But it was not until the 1970s, as older vessels became obsolete and newer ships were built, that the more versatile self-unloader began to edge out traditional "straight-deck" carriers for ore cargos as well.

Many straight-deckers were converted to self-unloaders (at considerable cost to the firms involved), while other vessels thought to have years of service ahead of them went to the scrapyard because they lacked self-unloading equipment. This trend was especially evident in the 1980s and resulted in the untimely demise of many fine lakers.

The aging of turn-of-the-century-vintage dockside unloading equipment found at various Great Lakes ports only hastened the end for the straight-decker. In 1992, the last of these "Hulett"-type unloading units was retired (although one remains standing in Cleveland and may be made into a museum).

As the Great Lakes shipping industry heads into the latter part of the 1990s, the only U.S.-flag, straight-deck bulk carriers in service are in the grain trade, however self-unloaders are making inroads there as well. On the Canadian side, straight-deckers may backhaul ore after delivering a grain cargo, but it is only a mater of time before virtually all cargo carried on lake boats will be carried on self-unloaders

Self-unloader Canadian Enterprise at work, unloading coal at Detroit's Zug Island complex.

Todd L. Davidson

Self-unloader Paul R. Tregurtha discharges coal at the Detroit Edison Recors Power Plant in the St. Clair River.

Philip A. Clayton

PASSAGES

The 1995 shipping season ended as it started - on ice. Late December brought an early freeze and ice conditions that were the worst in years at both ends of the Great Lakes (just ask the captains of the **Reserve** and **Indiana Harbor**, both of which grounded due to ice, and the crews of the cutters and tugs that kept the channels open). Despite setbacks due to the weather, the shipping industry enjoyed an exceptional year with almost all available vessels seeing service.

The same foul weather that brought early winter to the Great Lakes

Norris at Grand Haven, MI. *David Swain*

region also caused the year's most severe casualty on November 11 when a one-two combination of wind and seas at Port Colborne caused ULS Corporation's 1952-built self-unloader **James Norris** to hit a dock and sink. The Norris, the second-oldest operating Canadian laker, was repaired at Port Weller during the winter.

Perhaps the best news in years surrounds the re-activation of Oglebay-Norton's surplus self-unloader **J. Burton Ayers**, which has been deteriorating at Toledo since 1990. After an extensive re-fit at Sarnia, the 620-foot vessel was renamed **Cuyahoga** and placed in service by her new owners, Lower Lakes Towing Co. of Port Dover, Ontario *(See photos, page 22)*. With the sad parade of old lakers continuing their march to the scrapyard in recent years, this exception is nothing short of a miracle.

Fewer vessels than usual went to the boneyard in 1995, although as has often been the case, the demise of certain hulls seemed premature. Casualties included **Canadian Harvest** (ex-**Rimouski,** lost at sea on the way to a shipbreaker in India), **Canadian Pathfinder** (ex-**Baie St. Paul**), **Canadian Hunter, Algostream** (ex-**Simcoe**) and the tanker **LeFrene No. 1** (ex-**Jos. Simard**). Demolition also continued on **Lakewood**, **Beechglen** and the old crane boat **Buckeye**.

Another one-time Oglebay Norton self-unloader, the **Crispin Oglebay**, found a new life this year as a cargo transfer station at Hamilton. Appropriately renamed **Hamilton Transfer,** reports indicate she is less than a hit in her new role and may even return to powered service under the ULS Corporation flag.

Cont'd on Page 20

Inland Steel's absent Edward L. Ryerson, upbound near the Soo Locks, 16 July, 1991.

William P. Moran

Cont'd from Page 18

Also preparing for a new life is the long-laid-up passenger ship **Marine Star** (ex-**Aquarama**). This colorful lady of the lakes is at Buffalo, awaiting a new home in some port city willing to legalize waterborne casino gambling (the wait may be long). Also on the passenger ship scene, the former Bob-Lo Island steamers **Columbia** and **Ste. Claire** were sold in January, 1996, for historic preservation with the stated goal of returning at least one of the vintage ships to service.

Besides repairs to the crippled Norris, Port Weller Drydocks kept busy during the winter converting Algoma Central Marine's 14-year-old straight-decker **Capt. Henry Jackman** to a self-unloader. On the U.S. side, Bay Shipbuilding at Sturgeon Bay is building a 460-foot, self-unloading cement barge for the LaFarge interests with delivery scheduled for 1997. Boatwatchers are worried about the impact the "large LaFarge barge" will have on its venerable **E.M. Ford** of 1898, the oldest powered commercial vessel operating on the lakes.

Speaking of barges, **Sea Barge One**, the former American Steamship Co. self-unloader **Adam E. Cornelius**, enjoyed a busy 1995 on the lakes under charter to Canada Steamship Lines. Most observers thought that once the Cornelius was sold to Canadian East Coast interests in 1989 she had left the lakes for good.

Besides the **Cuyahoga**, several Fednav vessels had new names bestowed upon them in 1995, freeing up their former names for new vessels under construction. Hence, **Federal Saguenay** became **Federal Calliope**, **Federal St. Laurent** was rechristened **Federal Dora**, while the **Federal Maas** was renamed **Lake Michigan**.

Remaining out of service in 1995 (and probably for 1996 as well) was Inland Steel's much-loved bulk carrier **Edward L. Ryerson**, laid up at Sturgeon Bay, and Interlake's **J.L. Mauthe** and **John Sherwin**, in cold storage at Superior. Lack of self-unloading equipment has doomed these fine ore boats to inactivity.

Sea Barge One, upbound at the Soo, still looks like the laker she once was.

Jim Hoffman

James H. Neumiller

Canadian Pathfinder and Canadian Hunter at Toronto, just days before their overseas scrap tow.

'Don't Give Up the Ship ...'

FACING PAGE: *J. Burton Ayers gets a new coat of hull primer at Toledo before heading to Sarnia for re-fit. As work progressed she flew an appropriate banner ... 'Don't Give Up the Ship.'* (John R. Belliveau) THIS PAGE: **Back in service, Cuyahoga is downbound under the Blue Water Bridge at Port Huron on 14 November, 1995** (Dave Marcoux)

J.W. Westcott II makes her rounds. The Detroit fireboat Curtis Randolph is in the background.

'Mail by the Pail' delivers 100th

A Great Lakes tradition celebrated its centennial in 1995 when the J.W. Westcott Service, operator of the Detroit River mail boat, marked 100 years of delivering "mail by the pail."

Letters, magazines, newspapers, charts, supplies - even crewmembers who missed the boat at its last port of call - are the stock in trade for the 45-foot-*J.W. Westcott II,* docked on the U.S. side of the Detroit River under the Ambassador Bridge.

As David meets Goliath, the mail is passed up to waiting crew members via elaborately-painted buckets. The 'round-the-clock, nine-month-a-year service

Mail boat meets ore boat.

even has its own zip code - 48222. One hundred years ago, the mail was delivered from a rowboat; now the Westcott II relies on diesel power to effortlessly match speeds with vessels more than 20 times her size. On board the J. W. Westcott II, the postman's traditional credo is augmented by adding fog, ice, wind and waves to the time-honored delivery guarantee.

VESSEL INDEX

Vessel Name	Fleet No.	Vessel Name	Fleet No.	Vessel Name	Fleet No.
A		Apex Chicago	A-7	Blough, Roger	U-9
A-390	A-6	APT Mariner	F-3	Blue Nose	PM-4
A-397	A-6	Arctic	C-2	Boland, John J.	A-5
A-410	A-6	Arctic Ivik	F-3	Bond, Sir Robert	PM-4
Abegweit	PM-4	Arctic Kibvayok	F-3	Bounty	PV-2
Acacia	U-3	Arctic Kiggiak	F-3	Boyd, David	G-12
Adanac	P-6	Arctic Nanook	F-3	Bramble	U-3
Agawa Canyon	A-3	Arctic Nutsukpok	F-3	Bray, James M.	U-2
Agoming	T-1	Arctic Surveyor	F-3	Bristol Bay	U-3
Aird, John B.	A-3	Arizona	G-13	Brochu	F-2
Alabama	G-13	Arkansas	G-13	Buckeye	O-1
Alaska	G-13	Armco	O-1	Buckley	K-4
Alexander, Sir William	C-4	Asher, Chas	R-2	Buckthorn	U-3
Alexandria Belle	PU-1	Asher, John R.	R-2	Buffalo	A-5, U-2
Alexis Simard	A-2	Asher, Stephen M.	R-2	Buffalo Firefighter	B-10
Algocape	A-3	ASL Sanderling	F-3	Bunyan, Paul	U-2
Algocen	A-3	Atkinson, Arthur K.	PC-7	Burns Harbor	B-5
Algogulf	A-3	Atlantic Erie	C-3	Burro	M-4
Algoisle	A-3	Atlantic Freighter	PM-4	Burton, Courtney	O-1
Algolake	A-3	Atlantic Hickory	A-8	Busch, Gregory J.	B-11
Algomah	PA-4	Atlantic Superior	C-3	Busse, Fred A.	C-8
Algomarine	A-3	Atlantic Trader	C-3	**C**	
Algonorth	A-3	Atomic	M-11	C & O 452	C-12
Algontario	A-3	Aurora Borealis	PC-1	Cabot	F-3
Algoport	A-3	Avenger IV	P-6	Cadillac	PS-8
Algorail	A-3	**B**		Calcite II	U-9
Algoriver	A-3	B-7	A-6	California	G-13
Algosoo	A-3	B-16	A-6	Callaway, Cason J.	U-9
Algosound	A-3	Badger (43)	PL-1	Canadian Century	U-7
Algosteel	A-3	Bagotville	C-5	Canadian Empress	PS-1
Algoville	A-3	Baker, Melvin H., II	C-3	Canadian Enterprise	U-7
Algoway	A-3	Baldy B.	S-6	Canadian Explorer	U-7
Algowest	A-3	Barbara Rita	A-6	Canadian Leader	U-7
Algowood	A-3	Barker, James R.	I-4	Canadian Mariner	U-7
Alpena	I-2	Barker, Kaye E.	I-4	Canadian Miner	U-7
Ambassador	U-7	Barry J	K-5	Canadian Navigator	U-7
AMC 100	A-4	Bayfield	U-2	Canadian Olympic	U-7
American Girl	G-5	Bayship	B-4	Canadian Progress	U-7
American Mariner	A-5	Beaver	PU-2	Canadian Prospector	U-7
American Republic	A-5	Beaver D.	M-11	Canadian Provider	U-7
Amherst islander	PO-1	Beaver Islander	PB-1	Canadian Ranger	U-7
Amphibious	M-17	Bee Jay	G-2	Canadian Trader	U-7
Anchor Bay	G-11	Bernier, J. E.	C-4	Canadian Transport	U-7
Anderson, Arthur M.	U-9	Beeghly, Charles M.	I-4	Canadian Venture	U-7
Andre H.	T-6	Betty D.	D-5	Canadian Voyager	U-7
Andrew J.	G-4	Bide-A-Wee	PS-6	Capt. Barnaby	L-1
Andrie, Barbara	A-6	Bigane, Jos. F.	B-6	Capt. Ioannis S.	Q-2
Andrie, Candice	A-6	Billie M.	M-11	Capt. Roy	B-7
Andrie, Karen	A-6	Biscayne Bay	U-3	Capt. Shepler	PS-3
Andrie, Mari Beth	A-6	Blackie B.	E-1	Carey, Emmet J.	O-2
Anglian Lady	P-6	Block, Joseph L.	I-3	Caribbean Prince	PA-2
Antiquarian	G-12	Block, L. E.	B-3	Caribou	PM-4

Vessel Name	Fleet No.	Vessel Name	Fleet No.	Vessel Name	Fleet No.
Caribou Isle	C-4	Cort, Stewart J.	B-5	Durocher, Ray	D-5
Carl M.	C-7	Cotter, Edwin M.	B-10	**E**	
Carleton, George N.	G-8	Cove Isle	C-4	Earl Gray	C-4
Carol Ann	K-5	Crapo, S. T.	I-2	Eclipse	N-1
Carolyn Jo	M-11	CSL Atlas	C-3	Edelweiss I	PE-2
Cartier, Jacques	PC-2	CSL Cabo	C-3	Edelweiss II	PE-2
Cartierdoc	P-2	CSL Trillium	C-3	Edith J.	G-4
Cassidy, R. G.	G-8	CTC #1	M-13	Eighth Sea	S-1
Cavalier	R-1	Curly B.	L-1	El Lobo Grande II	G-13
Cedar Point	PC-3	Cuyahoga	L-4	Emerald Empress	PN-1
Cedar Point II	PC-3	**D**		Emerald Isle	PB-1
Cedar Point III	PC-3	Daldean	PB-3	Emery, John R.	E-5
Celebrezze, Anthony J.	C-9	Darrell, William	PH-2	Endeavor	PN-1
Cemba	M-3	Dauntless	M-12	Enerchem Asphalt	E-3
Challenger	PN-1	Day Peckinpaugh	E-5	Enerchem Catalyst	E-3
Champion	D-5, PC-4	DC 710	D-4	Enerchem Dolphin	E-3
Channel Cat	M-15	Dean, Americo	D-1	Enerchem Refiner	E-3
Charlevoix	PC-5	Dean, Anne M.	D-1	English River	C-3
Cherokee	B-2	Dean, Wayne	D-1	Erie Isle	PK-1, PP-1
Chi-Cheemaun	PO-2	Debbie Lyn	M-1	Erika Kobasic	B-3
Chicago's First Lady	PM-6	Defiance	A-4	Escort I	P-3
Chief Shingwauk	PL-3	Delaware	G-13	Escort II	P-3
Chief Wawatam	P-6	Des Groseilliers	C-4	Escorte	M-18
Chinook	M-15	des Jarnins, Alphonse	PS-5	Everest, D. C.	M-11
Chippewa	PA-4	Deschenes, Jos.	PS-5	Eyrarbakki	PW-3
Cicero	F-3	Desgagnes, Amelia	T-5	**F**	
Cisco	U-4	Desgagnes, Catherine	T-5	Fairchild	U-2
Citadel Hill	U-7	Desgagnes, Cecelia	T-5	Falcon, G. W.	L-1
City of Algonac	PW-2	Desgagnes, J. A. Z.	T-5	Farquharson, A. G.	S-8
City of Midland 41	PL-1	Desgagnes, Jacques	T-5	Federal Aalesund	F-3
City of Sandusky	PS-2	Desgagnes, Mathilda	T-5	Federal Agno	F-3
Clarke, Philip R.	U-9	Desgagnes, Melissa	T-5	Federal Baffin	F-3
Clifford, A. E.	PG-4	Desgagnes, Thalassa	T-5	Federal Bergen	F-3
Coastal Cruiser	T-1	Desmarais, Louis R.	C-3	Federal Calliope	F-3
Cohen, Wilfred M.	P-6	Detroit	N-2	Federal Dora	F-3
Coleman	U-2	Diamond Belle	PD-1	Federal Franklin	F-3
Colinette	W-1	Diamond Jack	PD-1	Federal Fraser	F-3
Colombe, J. E.	PU-2	Diamond Queen	PD-1	Federal Fuji	F-3
Colorado	G-13	Donald Bert	M-1	Federal Inger	F-3
Columbia	PS-9	Donald Mac	G-8	Federal Kumano	F-3
Columbia Star	O-1	Donald P.	Q-2	Federal Mackenzie	F-3
Columbus	B-1	Donner, William H.	U-8	Federal Manitou	F-3
Comeaudoc	P-2	Douglas, Sir John	C-4	Federal Matane	F-3
Commuter	PN-1	Dover Light	M-11	Federal Nord	F-3
Comorant	F-1	Drummond Islander	PE-1	Federal Oslo	F-3
Connecticut	G-13	Drummond Islander III	PE-1	Federal Pescadores	F-3
Confederation	PN-2	Duc D' Orleans	PD-3	Federal Polaris	F-3
Constructor	D-3	Duchess V	W-1	Federal Schelde	F-3
Cooper, Flo	P-4	Dufresne	M-11	Federal St. Clair	F-3
Cordillera	F-3	Duga	T-6	Federal St. Laurent	F-3
Cornelius, Adam E.	I-3	Duluth	U-2	Federal Vibeke	F-3
Corsair	PA-4	Dumit	C-4	Federal Vigra	F-3

ENAC

Roger LeLievre

Boatwatching up-close at the Welland Canal.

Vessel Name	Fleet No.	Vessel Name	Fleet No.	Vessel Name	Fleet No.
Felicia	M-9	**H**		Ile Des Barques	C-4
Felicity	PS-3	Hagen, Howard T.	M-7	Ile Ste. Ours	C-4
Ferbec	C-3	Halifax	C-3	Illinois	G-13
Flo-Mac	R-1	Halton	C-5	Imbeau, Armand	PS-5
Florida	G-13	Hamilton Energy	U-7	Imperial Acadia	I-1
Ford, E. M.	I-2	Hamilton Transfer	U-7	Imperial Bedford	I-1
Ford, J. B.	I-2	Hammond Bay	U-2, PL-2	Imperial Dartmouth	I-1
Forney	U-2	Handy Mariner	F-3	Imperial Lachine	I-1
Fourth Coast	S-1	Hannah 1801	H-3	Imperial St. Clair	I-1
Frankie D.	E-1	Hannah 1802	H-3	Indiana	G-13
Franklin, Sir John	C-4	Hannah 2801	H-3	Indiana Harbor	A-5
Frantz, Joseph H.	O-1	Hannah 2901	H-3	Inglis, William	PT-1
Fraser, Todd	F-5	Hannah 2902	H-3	Inland Seas	PI-1
Fraser, Simon	C-4	Hannah 2903	H-3	Iowa	G-13
Frederick, Owen M.	U-2	Hannah 3601	H-3	Irene, Shirley	PK-1
Frontenac	C-3	Hannah 5101	H-3	Iroquois	PI-2
Frontenac II	PO-1	Hannah, Daryl C.	H-3	Irving Arctic	K-3
G		Hannah, Donald C.	H-3	Irving Beech	A-8
G.L.B. No. 2	P-6	Hannah, Hannah D.	H-3	Irving Birch	A-8
G.T.B. 1	G-1	Hannah, James A.	H-3	Irving Canada	K-3
Gaucher, Hubert	S-8	Hannah, Kristen Lee	H-3	Irving Cedar	A-8
Gemini	C-10	Hannah, Mark	H-3	Irving Elm	A-8
General	D-5	Hannah, Mary E.	H-3	Irving Eskimo	K-3
Georgia	G-13	Hannah, Mary Page	H-3, S-6	Irving Maple	A-8
Georgios M.	F-3	Hannah, Peggy D.	H-3	Irving Ocean	K-3
Gilbert, Sir Humphrey	C-4	Hannah, Susan W.	H-3	Irving Timber	K-3
Gillen, Edward E., III	G-4	Harbor Master	R-3	Island Clipper	PV-2
Glen Shore	L-2	Harms, W. C.	G-7	Island Express	PA-4
Glenada	T-1	Harriman, Lewis G.	I-2	Island Gem	F-3
Glenbrook	M-11	Harris, James	L-1	Island Queen	PM-1
Glenevis	M-11	Harvey	U-2	Island Queen IV	PP-5
Glenora	PO-1	Henry T.	B-8	Island Skipper	F-3
Glenside	R-1	Hiawatha	PG-4, PS-6	Island Wanderer	PU-1
Goki	P-6	Highway 16	W-3	Islander	PM-7, PR-2
Goodtime I	PG-2	Hoey, Carolyn	G-1	Isle Royale Queen II	PK-2
Goodtime III	PG-3	Hoey, Patricia	G-1	**J**	
Gott, Edwin H.	U-9	Holiday	PS-6	J. G. II	M-4
Gouin, Lomer	PS-5	Holiday Island	PM-4	Jackman, Capt. Henry	A-3
Grand Island	PP-3	Holly Ann	H-4	Jackson, Charles E.	N-2
Grande Baie	A-2	Hope	PS-3	Jackson, Herbert C.	I-4
Grant, R. F.	T-6	Hope I	F-3	Jana	M-7
Gray, John Hamilton	PM-4	Horizon Montreal	S-7	Jarco 1402	R-3
Grayling	U-4	Houghton	U-2	Jason	M-7
Great Lakes	C-11	Hoyt, Elton, 2nd	I-4	Jerry G.	S-2
Greenstone	PU-2	Huron	U-2, PA-4	Jet Express	PP-7
Greta V	R-1	Huron Lady	PB-2	Jet Express II	PP-7
Gretchen B.	L-5	Husky 120	G-3	Jiggs	L-3
Griffith, H. M.	C-3	**I**		Jiimaan	PP-2
Griffon	C-4	Ian Mac	M-1	Joe Van	D-5
Grues Des Iles	PS-5	Icepurha	S-8	John Henry	K-5
Gull Isle	C-4	Idaho	G-13	John Joseph	A-6
		Iglehart, J. A. W.	I-2	Johnson	L-3

Vessel Name	Fleet No.	Vessel Name	Fleet No.	Vessel Name	Fleet No.
Johnson II	L-3	Laval	Q-2	Marine Star	PE-3
Johnson, Charles W.	P-6	Le Brave	Q-1	Marine Trader	A-1
Johnson, F. A.	G-8	Le Chene No. 1	S-8	Mariposa Belle	PM-5
Johnson, Martin E.	P-6	Le Gardeur, Catherine	PS-5	Marjolaine II	PC-8
Joliet	PS-8	Le Saule No. 1	S-8	Market, Wm.	PM-7
Judge McCombs	H-2	Le Survenant III	PC-9	Markus	U-2
Judy	M-15	Lee, Nancy A.	PL-2	Marlyn	PS-4
Julie Dee	K-5	Leitch, Gordon C.	U-7	Marquette	PS-8
Julio	J-1	Leonard W.	Q-2	Martin, Argue	R-1
K		LeVoyageur	PS-6	Maryland	G-13
Kadinger, David, Jr.	K-1	Limnos	C-1	Marysville	G-1
Kadinger, Ruffy J.	K-1	Linnhurst	F-1	Massachusetts	G-13
Kaho	U-4	Lord Selkirk	PN-2	Mauthe, J. L.	I-4
Kansas	G-13	Louie S.	R-2	Mayan Prince	PA-2
Kate B.	M-11	Louisiana	G-13	McAllister 132	P-6
Kathy Lynn	R-3	Lowell D.	PW-2	McAllister 252	M-11
Katie Ann	H-4	Lucien L.	PS-5	McAllister, Cathy	M-9
Katmai Bay	U-3	Ludington	K-5, U-2	McAllister, Daniel	M-9
Kaw	G-1	Luedtke, Alan K.	L-5	McAllister, Helen M.	M-9
Kelley Islander	PN-1	Luedtke, Chris E.	L-5	McAsphalt 401	M-10
Kellstone I	K-2	Luedtke, Erich R.	L-5	McBride, Sam	PT-1
Kenoki	C-4	Luedtke, Karl E.	L-5	McCarthy, Walter J., Jr.	A-5
Kenosha	U-2	Luedtke, Kurt	L-5	McCauley	U-2
Kentucky	G-13	Luedtke, Kurt R.	L-5	McGiffin, J. W.	C-3
Keta V.	V-1	Luedtke, Paul L.	L-5	McGrath, James E.	U-7
Kinsman Enterprise	K-6	**M**		McKee Sons	U-8
Kinsman Independent	K-6	Mackenzie, William Lyon	T-3	McKeil, Evans B.	M-11
Kristen D.	PP-4	Mackie, Douglas B.	G-9	McKeller	P-6
Krystal K.	B-3	Mackinac Express	PA-4	Meaghan Beth	D-5
L		Mackinaw	U-3	Medill, Joseph	C-8
L' Orme No. 1	S-8	Madeline	PM-1	Medusa Challenger	M-13
L.S.C. 236	G-1	Magnetic	F-4	Medusa Conquest	M-13
La Salle	PS-8	Maid of the Mist	PM-2	Mesabi Miner	I-4
Lac Como	M-11	Maid of the Mist III	PM-2	Metis	E-8
Lac Erie	M-11	Maid of the Mist IV	PM-2	Michigan C-11, G-13, U-2	
Lac Manitoba	M-11	Maid of the Mist V	PM-2	Middletown	O-1
Lac Vancouver	M-11	Maid of the Mist VI	PM-2	Midstate I	S-5
Lake Carling	F-3	Maid of the Mist VII	PM-2	Midstate II	S-5
Lake Champlain	F-3	Maine	G-13	Miller, William M.	PM-7
Lake Charles	F-3	Malabar	PT-2	Miners Castle	PP-3
Lake Erie	F-3	Malden	P-6	Minnesota	G-13
Lake Guardian	U-5	Manitou M-2, PA-3, PT-2		Miseford	P-6
Lake Michigan	F-3	Manitou Island	PM-3	Mishe-Mokwa	PM-3
Lake Ontario	F-3	Manitoulin	C-3	Miss Brockville	PU-3
Lake Superior	F-3, U-2	Manitowoc M-8, U-2		Miss Brockville IV	PU-3
Langton, J. G.	T-4	Mantadoc	P-2	Miss Brockville V	PU-3
Lansdowne	PS-7	Mapleglen	P-1	Miss Brockville VI	PU-3
Lapish, Art	L-1	Marcey	M-4	Miss Brockville VII	PU-3
Laud, Sam	A-5	Marcoux, Camille	PS-5	Miss Brockville VIII	PU-3
Laura Lynn	H-4	Margaret Ann	H-4	Miss Clayton III	PU-1
Laurentian	M-16	Marine Evangeline	PM-4	Miss Clayton IV	PU-1
Laurier, Sir Wilfred	C-4	Marine Hunter	F-3	Miss Edna	K-5

Vessel Name	Fleet No.	Vessel Name	Fleet No.	Vessel Name	Fleet No.
Miss Ivy Lea II	PI-3	Mississippi	G-13	Montmagny	C-4
Miss Ivy Lea III	PI-3	Missouri	G-13	Montmorency	C-4
Miss Midland	PP-5	Mobile Bay	U-3	Montrealais	U-7
Miss Montreal	PC-6	Moby Dick	S-6	Moore, Olive M.	U-8
Miss Munising	PP-3	Montana	G-13	Morgan	K-4
Miss Superior	PP-3	Montcalm	C-4	Morton Salt 74	M-19

David Maize

George A. Stinson, shown under M.A. Hanna colors, upbound at Port Huron.

Vessel Name	Fleet No.	Vessel Name	Fleet No.	Vessel Name	Fleet No.
Mosdeep	F-3	Offshore Supplier	M-11	Presque Isle	U-9
Mott, Charlie	PU-2	Oglebay Norton	O-1	Pride of Michigan	U-6
Mr. Micky	H-1	Oglebay, Earl W.	O-1	Prince Edward	PN-2
Munson, John G.	U-9	Ohio	G-13	Prince Nova	PN-2
Muskegon	K-5	Oil Queen	G-5	Princess of Acadia	PM-4
Musky II	U-4	Ojibway	U-9	Provider	PG-4
N		Oklahoma	G-13	Provmar Terminal	U-7
Nahidik	C-4	Old Mission	K-4	Provmar Terminal II	U-7
Nancy Anne	D-5	Oldendorff, Bernard	C-3	Provo Wallis	C-4
Nanticoke	C-3	Oldendorff, Christopher	C-3	Purves, John	A-6
Narwhal	C-4	Omni Sorel	M-9	Purvis, W. I. Scott	P-6
Natchitoches	U-2	Omni-Richlieu	S-9	Purvis, W. J. Ivan	P-6
Nathan S.	M-5	Omni-St. Laurent	S-9	**Q**	
Neah Bay	U-3	Ongiara	PT-1	Quebecois	U-7
Nebraska	G-13	Ontamich	PB-3	Quedoc	P-2
Neebish Islander	PE-1	Oregon	G-13	Queen of Andersonville	PW-4
Neebish Islander II	PE-1	Osborne, F. M.	O-2	**R**	
Nelvana	U-7	Oshawa	C-7	R. & L. No. 1	G-10
Neptune III	D-1	Ottawa	PA-4	R.C. L. No. 11	C-5
Nevada	G-13	Outer Island	E-4	Racine	U-2
Neville, Gerald D.	PD-2	**P**		Radisson	PS-5, PS-8
New Hampshire	G-13	P.M.L. Alton	P-6	Radisson, Pierre	C-4
New Jersey	G-13	P.M.L. Salvager	P-6	Randolph, Curtiss	D-2
New Mexico	G-13	Paj	U-2	Ranger III	PU-2
New York	G-13	Palladino, Frank, Jr.	K-2	Reiss Marine	M-6
Newberry, Jerry	M-11	Parisien, Jean	C-3	Reiss, Richard	E-7
Niagara II	M-11	Paterson	P-2	Rennie, Thomas	PT-1
Niagara Prince	PA-2	Paul E. No. 1	M-11	Reserve	O-1
Nichevo II	PM-1	Paula M.	C-5	Rest, William	T-4
Nicolet	A-5, U-2, PS-8	Payette, Thomas A.	L-4	Rhode Island	G-13
Nindawayma	PO-2	PBI No. 1	P-3	Richmond Hill	U-7
No. 4	R-3	Pelee Islander	PP-2	Richter, C. G.	PW-3
No. 25	H-3	Peninsula	G-8	Rickey, James W.	D-3
No. 26	H-3	Pennsylvania	G-13	Ridgeway, Benjamin	K-2
No. 28	H-3	Pere Marquette 10	C-12	Risley, Samuel	C-4
No. 29	H-3	Pete, C. West	U-1	Roanoke	M-8
No. 66-4	N-1	Petite Forte	G-10	Robert B. No. 1	R-1
Noble, Robert	PW-3	Petka	F-3	Robert H.	T-6
Nokomis	PS-6	Pictured Rocks	PP-3	Robert John	G-8
Nordic Blossom	E-3	Pioneer	U-7	Robert W.	T-1
Nordik Express	T-5	Plainsville	R-1	Robinson Bay	S-1
Nordik Passeur	T-5	Point Carroll	E-2	Rocket	P-6
Norma B.	F-4	Point Chebucto	E-2	Roman, Stephen B.	E-8
Norris, James	U-7	Point Halifax	E-2	Rosalee D.	T-1
North Carolina	G-13	Point Valour	T-2	Rouge	U-2
North Channel	PC-4	Point Vibert	E-2	Ryerson, Edward L.	I-3
North Dakota	G-13	Point Vigour	E-2	**S**	
Northwestern	G-11	Point Vim	E-2	S.M.T.B. No. 7	M-11
Norton, David Z.	O-1	Pointe Aux Basques	E-2	Sacre Bleu	PS-3
O		Pointe Comeau	E-2	Saguenay	C-3
Oakglen	P-1	Pointe Sept Iles	E-2	Salty Dog 1	M-11
Oatka	A-1	Port City Princess	PP-6	Salvage Monarch	M-9

Downbound Montrealais meets upbound Cason J. Callaway near St. Clair, MI., 4 August, 1995.

Vessel Name	Fleet No.	Vessel Name	Fleet No.	Vessel Name	Fleet No.
Sand Pebble	K-7	Stanley	U-2	**U**	
Sandpiper	PH-1	STC 2004	B-11	Uncle Sam	PU-1
Saskatchewan Pioneer	C-3	Ste. Claire	PS-10	Uncle Sam VI	PU-1
Saturn	C-10	Ste. Marie I	PP-5	Uncle Sam VII	PU-1
Sauniere	A-3	Steelhead	M-15	Upper Canada	PP-2
Savard, Joseph	PS-5	Stella Borealis	PR-1	Utah	G-13
Scandrett, Fred	T-4	Stinson, George A.	I-4	**V**	
Schlaegar, Victor L.	C-8	Stormont	M-11	Vacationland	PM-4
Schwartz, H. J.	U-2	Straits Express	PA-4	Vachon	F-2
Scotia II	C-6	Straits of Mackinac II	PA-4	Vacy Ash, W. M.	Q-1
Sea Barge One	C-3	Su-Joy III	F-5	Vandoc	P-2
Sea Castle	A-6	Sugar Islander II	PE-1	Venture	R-3
Sea Eagle II	S-3	Sundew	U-3	Vermont	G-13
Sea Queen II	PA-3	Superior	G-13	Viking	PC-7
Seaway Queen	U-7	Sykes, Wilfred	I-3	Virginia	G-13
Segwun	PM-8			Vista King	PV-1
Selvick, Bonnie G.	S-6	**T**		Vista Star	PV-1
Selvick, Carl William	S-6	2361	L-3	Voyager	PW-3
Selvick, Carla Anne	S-6	3403	L-3	Voyageur II	PG-4
Selvick, John M.	S-6	Tadoussac	C-3	**W**	
Selvick, Sharon M.	S-6	Tarantau	C-3	Wack, Otis	M-11
Selvick, William C.	S-6	Taverner	PM-4	Walpole Islander	PW-2
Shannon	G-1	Tawas Bay	U-2	Washington G-13, U-2,	PW-3
Shelter Bay	U-2	Taylor, Myron C.	U-9	Wellington Kent	K-3
Sherwin, John	I-4	Tennessee	G-13	Wendella Clipper	PW-4
Shoreline	PS-4	Texas	G-13	Wendella Limited	PW-4
Sillery	M-11	The Howe Islander	PH-3	Wendella Sunliner	PW-4
Simcoe	C-4	The Quinte Loyalist	PO-1	Wenonah	PG-4
Simons, Roger R.	U-5	Thompson, Joseph H.	U-8	West Shore	PM-7
Simonsen	U-2	Thompson, Joseph H., Jr.	U-8	Westcott, J. W., II	W-2
Sinmac	M-9	Thornhill	U-7	Whitby	C-7
Siscowet	U-4	Thousand Islander	PG-1	White, Fred R., Jr.	O-1
Skyline Princess	PM-6	Thousand Islander II	PG-1	White, H. Lee	A-5
Skyline Queen	PM-6	Thousand Islander III	PG-1	Whitefish Bay	U-2
Sloan, George A.	U-9	Thousand Islander IV	PG-1	Willmac	M-11
Smallwood, Joseph & Clara	PM-4	Thunder Bay	PE-1	Willowglen	G-6
Smith, H. A.	G-3	Timmy A.	R-2	Wilson, Charles E.	A-5
Solta	F-3	Toledo	M-11	Windoc	P-2
South Bass	PM-7	Tonawanda	R-3	Windsor	M-8
South Carolina	G-13	Toni D.	P-5	Winnebago	J-1
South Channel	PC-4	Torontonian	PA-1	Wisconsin	G-13
South Shore	PB-1	Townsend, Paul H.	I-2	Witch	D-5
Spartan (42)	PL-1	Tracy	C-4	Wolf River	G-8
Speer, Edgar B.	U-9	Tregurtha, Lee A.	I-4	Wolfe Islander III	PO-1
Spence, John	M-11	Tregurtha, Paul R.	I-4	Wolverine	G-11, O-1
Spuds	R-2	Trillium	PT-1	Wyoming	G-13
St. Clair	A-5, C-6	Trinidad	PW-1		
St. Clair Flats	PC-4	Triton	M-14	**Y**	
St. John, J. S.	E-6	Trois Rivieres	PS-5	Yankcanuck	P-6
St. Mary's Cement	S-4	Tug Malcom	M-2	Yankee Clipper	PP-1, PV-2
St. Mary's Cement II	S-3	Tupper	C-4	Yorke, Margaret	C-6
St. Mary's Cement III	S-3	Twolan, W. N.	B-9	Yorke, Phyllis	C-6

FLEET & SHIP LISTINGS

Kinsman Enterprise loads grain at Superior, 6 May, 1995

Mike Sipper

FLEET & SHIP LISTINGS

Listed after each vessel in order are type of ship, year built, type of vessel, tonnage in carrying capacity, overall length, beam and depth. The figures given are as accurate as possible and are provided for informational purposes only. Note: tugs, excursion ships, Coast Guard vessels and other miscellaneous ships are given in gross tons. Tanker capacities are in barrels.

For your convenience, the following abbreviations have been used.

AC	Auto Carrier	DR	Dredge	PK	Package Freighter
BB	Bum Boat	ES	Excursion Ship	RR	Roll On/Roll Off
BC	Bulk Carrier	FB	Fire Boat	RT	Restaurant
BRIG	Brigantine	FD	Floating Dry Dock	RV	Research Vessel
BT	Buoy Tender	GL	Gate Lifter	SB	Supply Boat
CB	Crane Barge	GU	Grain Self Unloader	SC	Sand Carrier
CC	Cement Carrier	IB	Ice Breaker	SS	Submarine
CF	Car Ferry	LS	Lightship	SU	Self Unloader
CLG	Cruiser	MB	Mail Boat	SV	Survey Vessel
CS	Crane Ship	PA	Passenger Vessel	TB	Tug Boat
DB	Deck Barge	PB	Pilot Boat	TF	Train Ferry
DD	Destoyer	PF	Passenger Ferry	TK	Tanker
DD	Destroyer			TV	Training Vessel
ER	Environmental Response Ship				

PROPULSION

B	Barge	Q	Steam - Quad. Expansion	SAIL	
BT	Batteries	R	Steam - Triple Expansion	T	Steam - Turbine
D	Diesel	S	Steam - Skinner Uniflow	U	Steam - Uniflow
L	Steam - Lentz Poppet Quad. Expansion				

Fleet No. and Name Vessel Name	Year Built	Type of Ship	Type of Engine	Cargo Cap. or Gross*	Length	Beam	Depth or Draft*
A-1 — ACME TUG SERVICE, DULUTH, MN							
Marine Trader	1939	BB	D	67*	65' 00"	15' 00"	7' 06"
Oatka	1934	TB	D	12*	40' 00"	10' 00"	4' 00"
A-2 — ALCAN SMELTERS & CHEMICALS LTD., PORT ALFRED, PQ							
Grande Baie	1972	TB	D	194*	86' 06"	30' 00"	12' 00"
Alexis Simard	1980	TB	D	286*	92' 00"	34' 00"	13' 07"
A-3 — ALGOMA CENTRAL MARINE, SAULT STE. MARIE, ON							
Agawa Canyon	1970	SU	D	23,400	647' 00"	72' 00"	40' 00"
John B. Aird	1983	SU	D	31,300	730' 00"	75' 10"	46' 06"
Algocape	1967	BC	D	29,950	730' 00"	75' 00"	39' 08"
(Richelieu '67 - '94)							
Algocen	1968	BC	D	28,400	730' 00"	75' 00"	39' 08"
Algogulf	1961	BC	T	26,950	730' 00"	75' 00"	39' 00"
(J. N. McWatters '61 - '91, Scott Misener '91 - '94)							

Fleet No. and Name / Vessel Name	Year Built	Type of Ship	Type of Engine	Cargo Cap. or Gross*	Length	Beam	Depth or Draft*
Algoisle	1963	BC	D	26,700	730' 00"	75' 00"	39' 03"
(Silver Isle '63 - '94)							
Algolake	1977	BC	D	32,150	730' 00"	75' 00"	46' 06"
Algomarine	1968	SU	D	27,000	730' 00"	75' 00"	39' 08"
(Lake Manitoba '68 - '87)							
Algonorth	1971	BC	D	28,000	729' 09"	75' 02"	42' 11"
(Temple Bar '71 - '77, Lake Nipigon '77 - '84, Laketon '84 - '86, Lake Nipigon '86 - '87)							
Algontario	1960	BC	D	29,100	730' 00"	75' 09"	40' 02"
(Ruhr Ore '60 - '76, Cartiercliffe Hall '76 - '88, Winnipeg '88 - '94)							
Algoport	1979	SU	D	32,000	658' 00"	75' 10"	46' 06"
Algorail	1968	SU	D	23,750	640' 05"	72' 03"	40' 00"
Algoriver	1960	BC	T	26,800	722' 06"	75' 00"	39' 00"
(John A. France '60 - '94)							
Algosoo	1974	SU	D	31,300	730' 00"	75' 00"	44' 06"
Algosound	1965	BC	T	27,700	730' 00"	75' 00"	39' 00"
(Don-De-Dieu '65 - '67, V. W. Scully '67 - '87)							
Algosteel	1966	SU	D	27,000	730' 00"	75' 00"	39' 08"
(A. S. Glossbrenner '66 - '87, Algogulf '87 - '90)							
Algoville	1967	BC	D	28,200	730' 00"	75' 00"	39' 08"
(Senneville '67 - '94)							
Algoway	1972	SU	D	24,000	650' 00"	72' 00"	40' 00"
Algowest	1982	BC	D	33,300	730' 00"	75' 10"	42' 00"
Algowood	1981	SU	D	31,750	730' 00"	75' 10"	46' 06"
Capt. Henry Jackman	1981	SU	D	31,800	730' 00"	75' 10"	42' 00"
(Lake Wabush '81 - '87)							

NAVIGATION SONAMAR — MANAGED

Sauniere	1970	SU	D	23,900	642' 10"	74' 10"	42' 00"
(Brooknes '70 - '76, Algosea '76 - '82)							

NEW VESSELS

New Building	1997	BC	D	48,700	650' 00"	100' 00"	60' 00"
New Building	1997	BC	D	48,700	650' 00"	100' 00"	60' 00"

A-4 — AMERICAN MARINE CONSTRUCTORS, ST. JOSEPH, MI

Defiance	1966	TB	D	26*	44' 08"	18' 00"	6' 00"
AMC 100	1978	DB	B	1,237	200' 00"	53' 00"	11' 06"

A-5 — AMERICAN STEAMSHIP CO., WILLIAMSVILLE, NY

American Mariner	1980	SU	D	37,200	730' 00"	78' 00"	45' 00"
American Republic	1981	SU	D	24,800	634' 10"	68' 00"	40' 00"
John J. Boland	1953	SU	T	20,200	639' 03"	72' 00"	36' 00"
Buffalo	1978	SU	D	23,800	634' 10"	68' 00"	40' 00"
Indiana Harbor	1979	SU	D	78,850	1,000' 00"	105' 00"	56' 00"
Sam Laud	1975	SU	D	23,800	634' 10"	68' 00"	40' 00"
Walter J. McCarthy Jr.	1977	SU	D	78,850	1,000' 00"	105' 00"	56' 00"
(Belle River '77 - '90)							
Nicolet	1905	SU	D	11,150	533' 00"	60' 00"	31' 00"
(William G. Mather '05 - '25, J. H. Sheadle '25 - '55, H. L. Gobeille '55 - '65)							
(Last operated December 27, 1990 — Currently laid up in Toledo, OH)							
St. Clair	1976	SU	D	44,000	770' 00"	92' 00"	52' 00"
H. Lee White	1974	SU	D	35,200	704' 00"	78' 00"	45' 00"
Charles E. Wilson	1973	SU	D	33,800	680' 00"	78' 00"	45' 00"

Fleet No. and Name Vessel Name	Year Built	Type of Ship	Type of Engine	Cargo Cap. or Gross*	Length	Beam	Depth or Draft*
A-6 — ANDRIE, INC., MUSKEGON, MI							
Barbara Andrie	1940	TB	D	298*	121' 10"	29' 06"	16' 00"
Barbara Rita		TB	D		36' 00"	14' 00"	6' 00"
John Joseph	1993	TB	D		40' 00"	14' 00"	5' 00"
John Purves	1919	TB	D	436*	150' 00"	27' 07"	16' 00"
Karen Andrie	1965	TB	D	433*	120' 00"	31' 06"	16' 00"
Mari Beth Andrie	1961	TB	D	147*	87' 00"	24' 00"	11' 06"
Candice Andrie	1958	CB	B	1,000	150' 00"	52' 00"	10' 00"
A-390	1982	TK	B	39,000	310' 00"	60' 00"	19' 03"
A-397	1993	TK	B	39,700	270' 00"	60' 00"	25' 00"
A-410	1971	TK	B	41,000	335' 00"	54' 00"	26' 06"
B-7	1976	DB	B	1,350	165' 00"	42' 06"	12' 00"
B-16	1976	DB	B	1,350	165' 00"	42' 06"	12' 00"
Sea Castle	1909	CC	B	2,600	260' 00"	43' 00"	25' 03"

(Kaministiquia '09 - '16, Westoil '16 - '23, J. B. John '23 - '51, John L. A. Galster '51 - '69)
(Currently laid up in Muskegon, MI)

A-7 — APEX OIL CO., FORESTVIEW, IL							
Apex Chicago	1981	TK	B	35,000	288' 00"	60' 00"	19' 00"
A-8 — ATLANTIC TOWING LTD., SAINT JOHN, NB							
Atlantic Hickory	1973	TB	D	912*	145' 00"	38' 09"	21' 02"
Irving Beech	1983	TB	D	294*	104' 02"	30' 03"	13' 02"
Irving Birch	1967	TB	D	827*	162' 03"	38' 02"	19' 08"
Irving Cedar	1974	TB	D	492*	151' 01"	35' 06"	17' 08"
Irving Elm	1980	TB	D	427*	116' 01"	31' 06"	18' 08"
Irving Maple	1966	TB	D	487*	126' 03"	32' 06"	17' 04"
B-1 — B+B DREDGING CORP., CRYSTAL RIVER, FL							
Columbus	1944	DR	D	2,923*	310' 02"	50' 00"	22' 01"

(USS LST 987 '44 - '55, USS Millard County (LST 987) '55 - '73, Esperance III '73 - '86)

B-2 — BARGE TRANSPORTATION, INC., DETROIT, MI							
Cherokee	1947	DB	B	1,200	155' 00"	50' 00"	13' 06"
B-3 — BASIC TOWING, INC., ESCANABA, MI							
L. E. Block	1927	BC	T	15,900	621' 00"	64' 00"	33' 00"

(Last operated October 31, 1981 — Currently laid up in Escanaba, MI)

Erika Kobasic	1939	TB	D	226*	110' 00"	27' 00"	15' 00"
Krystal K.	1943	TB	D	493*	133' 00"	33' 00"	17' 00"
B-4 — BAY SHIPBUILDING CORP., STURGEON BAY, WI							
Bayship	1943	TB	D	19*	45' 00"	12' 06"	6' 00"
B-5 — BETHLEHEM STEEL CORP., GREAT LAKES STEAMSHIP DIV., CHESTERTON, IN							
Burns Harbor	1980	SU	D	78,850	1,000' 00"	105' 00"	56' 00"
Stewart J. Cort	1972	SU	D	58,000	1,000' 00"	105' 00"	49' 00"
B-6 — BIGANE VESSEL FUELING CO., CHICAGO, IL							
Jos. F. Bigane	1973	TK	D	7,500	140' 00"	40' 00"	14' 00"

Roger LeLievre

ULS Corporation's Canadian Century on the Welland Canal, 18 July, 1995.

Fleet No. and Name Vessel Name	Year Built	Type of Ship	Type of Engine	Cargo Cap. or Gross*	Length	Beam	Depth or Draft*
B-7 — BRIAN UTILITIES SERVICES, INC., MUSKEGON, MI							
Capt. Roy	1987	TB	D	27*	42' 06"	12' 08"	6' 06"
B-8 — LE BRUN CONSTRUCTORS LTD., THUNDER BAY, ON							
Henry T.	1932	DB	B	1,000	120' 00"	44' 00"	11' 00"
B-9 — BUCHANAN FOREST PRODUCTS, THUNDER BAY, ON							
W. N. Twolan	1962	TB	D	299*	106' 00"	29' 00"	14' 00"
B-10 — CITY OF BUFFALO DEPT. OF FIRE, BUFFALO, NY							
Buffalo Firefighter		FB	D		106' 00"	24' 00"	11' 00"
Edwin M. Cotter	1900	FB	D	188*	106' 00"	24' 00"	11' 00"
B-11 — BUSCH OCEANOGRAPHIC EQUIPMENT CO., SAGINAW, MI							
Gregory J. Busch	1919	TB	D	299*	151' 00"	28' 00"	16' 09"
STC 2004	1986	DB	B	2,364	240' 00"	50' 00"	9' 05"
C-1 — CANADA CENTRE FOR INLAND WATERS, BURLINGTON, ON							
Limnos	1968	RV	D	460*	147' 00"	32' 00"	8' 06"
C-2 — GOVERNMENT OF CANADA, OTTAWA, ON							
Arctic	1978	BC	D	28,000	692' 04"	75' 05"	49' 05"
C-3 — CANADA STEAMSHIP LINES, INC., MONTREAL, PQ							
Louis R. Desmarais	1977	SU	D	33,000	730' 00"	75' 00"	46' 06"
Frontenac	1968	SU	D	27,500	729' 07"	75' 03"	39' 08"
H. M. Griffith	1973	SU	D	31,250	730' 00"	75' 00"	46' 06"
Halifax	1963	SU	T	30,100	730' 00"	75' 00"	39' 03"
(Frankcliffe Hall '63 - '88)							
Manitoulin	1966	SU	D	28,100	730' 00"	75' 00"	41' 00"
J. W. McGiffin	1972	SU	D	33,100	730' 00"	75' 00"	46' 06"
Nanticoke	1980	SU	D	35,100	730' 00"	75' 08"	46' 06"
Jean Parisien	1977	SU	D	33,000	730' 00"	75' 00"	46' 06"
Saguenay	1964	SU	D	30,500	730' 00"	75' 02"	44' 08"
(Last operated November 30, 1992 — Currently laid up in Toronto, ON)							
Tadoussac	1969	SU	D	29,700	730' 00"	75' 03"	42' 00"
Tarantau	1965	SU	T	27,600	730' 00"	75' 00"	46' 06"
CSL INTERNATIONAL							
Atlantic Erie	1985	SU	D	38,200	736' 06"	75' 10"	50' 00"
(Hon. Paul Martin '85 - '88)							
Atlantic Superior	1982	SU	D	38,900	730' 00"	75' 10"	50' 00"
Melvin H. Baker II	1984	SU	D	34,600	736' 06"	75' 10"	46' 06"
(Prairie Harvest '84 - '89, Atlantic Huron '89 - '94)							
CSL Atlas	1990	SU	D	68,000	747' 05"	105' 00"	60' 00"
CSL Cabo	1986	SU	D	68,000	740' 00"	105' 00"	60' 00"
Ferbec	1979	BC	D	60,000	747' 00"	105' 00"	60' 00"
Bernard Oldendorff	1991	SU	D	77,000	747' 00"	105' 00"	60' 00"
Christopher Oldendorff	1982	SU	D	63,000	747' 00"	105' 00"	60' 00"
(Pacific Peace '82 - '86, Atlantic Huron '86 - '88, CSL Innovator '88 - '94)							
ALGOMA CENTRAL MARINE — CHARTERED							
Atlantic Trader	1978	SU	D	34,900	730' 00"	75' 10"	46' 06"
(Algobay '78 - '94)							

Fleet No. and Name Vessel Name	Year Built	Type of Ship	Type of Engine	Cargo Cap. or Gross*	Length	Beam	Depth or Draft*
HALIFAX GRAIN ELEVATORS LTD. — CHARTERED							
Sea Barge One	1959	SU	B	23,200	611" 03"	72' 00"	40' 00"
(Adam E. Cornelius '59 - '89, Capt. Edward V. Smith '89 - '91)							
LAFARGE CANADA, INC. — MANAGED							
English River	1961	CC	D	7,450	404' 03"	60' 00"	36' 06"
New Building	1997	CC	B	14,000	460' 00"	70' 00"	37' 00"
PIONEER SHIPPING LTD. — MANAGED							
Saskatchewan Pioneer	1983	BC	D	34,500	730' 00"	75' 09"	48' 00"
ST. LAWRENCE CEMENT CO. — MANAGED							
CSL Trillium		CC	B	18,064			
(Pacnav Princess - '94)							
NEW VESSELS							
Hull 2227	1997	SU	D	70,800	734' 11"	105' 00"	63' 00"
Hull 2228	1997	SU	D	70,800	734' 11"	105' 00"	63' 00"
Hull 2229	1998	SU	D	70,800	734' 11"	105' 00"	63' 00"

C-4 — CANADIAN COAST GUARD, GREAT LAKES FLEET, OTTAWA, ON

Sir William Alexander	1986	IB	D	3,550*	272' 06"	45' 00"	17' 06"
J. E. Bernier	1963	IB	D	3,150*	231' 04"	48' 11"	16' 00"
Des Groseilliers	1982	IB	D	5,910*	322' 00"	64' 00"	23' 06"
Sir John Franklin	1980	IB	D	5,034*	332' 00"	64' 00"	23' 06"
Simon Fraser	1960	IB	D	1,352*	210' 00"	42' 00"	18' 03"
Sir Humphrey Gilbert	1959	IB	D	1,620*	220' 06"	48' 06"	16' 03"
Griffon	1970	IB	D	2,828*	234' 00"	49' 00"	21' 06"
Sir Wilfred Laurier	1986	IB	D	3,812*	272' 04"	53' 02"	25' 05"
Montcalm	1957	IB	D	2,094*	220' 06"	48' 03"	16' 05"
Pierre Radisson	1978	IB	D	5,910*	322' 07"	65' 01"	35' 05"
Tracy	1968	IB	D	1,300*	182' 00"	38' 00"	16' 00"
Tupper	1959	IB	D	1,871*	204' 06"	42' 00"	14' 00"
Caribou Isle	1986	BT	D	92*	75' 05"	19' 07"	7' 04"
Cove Isle	1980	BT	D	80*	65' 07"	19' 08"	7' 04"
Sir John Douglas	1956	BT	D	564*	151' 04"	31' 03"	13' 05"
Dumit	1979	BT	D	569*	167' 09"	41' 05"	9' 02"
Earl Gray	1986	BT	D	1,971*	230' 00"	46' 02"	22' 01"
Gull Isle	1980	BT	D	80*	65' 07"	19' 08"	7' 04"
Ile Des Barques		BT	D	139*	75' 06"	19' 07"	4' 07"
Ile Ste. Ours		BT	D	139*	75' 06"	19' 07"	4' 07"
Kenoki	1964	BT	D	275*	108' 11"	32' 02"	6' 03"
Montmagny	1963	BT	D	625*	148' 00"	28' 10"	8' 06"
Montmorency	1957	BT	D	1,006*	165' 00"	34' 00"	15' 00"
Nahidik	1974	BT	D	856*	176' 05"	50' 08"	10' 05"
Narwhal	1963	BT	D	2,064*	253' 01"	43' 02"	21' 07"
Samuel Risley	1985	BT	D	1,988*	228' 09"	47' 01"	21' 09"
Simcoe	1962	BT	D	961*	179' 03"	38' 00"	15' 06"
Provo Wallis	1969	BT	D	1,383*	190' 04"	41' 02"	16' 08"

C-5 — CANADIAN DREDGE & DOCK, INC., DON MILLS, ON

Bagotville	1964	TB	D	65*	65' 00"	18' 06"	10' 00"
Halton	1942	TB	D	15*	42' 09"	14' 00"	7' 06"
Paula M.	1959	TB	D	12*	46' 06"	16' 01"	4' 10"
R.C. L. No. 11	1958	TB	D	20*	42' 09"	14' 03"	5' 09"

Fleet No. and Name / Vessel Name	Year Built	Type of Ship	Type of Engine	Cargo Cap. or Gross*	Length	Beam	Depth or Draft*

C-6 — CANADIAN NATIONAL RAILWAYS, SARNIA, ON

Vessel Name	Year Built	Type of Ship	Type of Engine	Cargo Cap. or Gross*	Length	Beam	Depth or Draft*
Margaret Yorke	1970	TB	D	272*	99' 00"	35' 00"	6' 00"
Phyllis Yorke	1970	TB	D	272*	99' 00"	35' 00"	6' 00"
St. Clair	1927	TF	B	27 rail cars	400' 00"	54' 00"	22' 00"
(Pere Marquette 12 '27 - '70)							
Scotia II	1915	TF	B	16 rail cars	300' 00"	48' 03"	18' 02"

(All last operated April 4, 1995 — All currently laid up in Sarnia, ON)

C-7 — CARTIER CONSTRUCTION CO., BELLEVILLE, ON

Vessel Name	Year Built	Type of Ship	Type of Engine	Cargo Cap. or Gross*	Length	Beam	Depth or Draft*
Carl M.	1957	TB	D	21*	47' 00"	14' 06"	6' 00"
Oshawa	1971	TB	D	24*	45' 00"	14' 00"	5' 00"
Whitby	1978	TB	D	24*	45' 00"	14' 00"	5' 00"

C-8 — CHICAGO FIRE DEPT., CHICAGO, IL

Vessel Name	Year Built	Type of Ship	Type of Engine	Cargo Cap. or Gross*	Length	Beam	Depth or Draft*
Fred A. Busse	1937	FB	D	209*	92' 00"	23' 00"	8' 00"
Joseph Medill	1949	FB	D	209*	92' 00"	23' 00"	8' 00"
Victor L. Schlaegar	1949	FB	D	209*	92' 00"	23' 00"	8' 00"

C-9 — CLEVELAND FIRE DEPT., CLEVELAND, OH

Vessel Name	Year Built	Type of Ship	Type of Engine	Cargo Cap. or Gross*	Length	Beam	Depth or Draft*
Anthony J. Celebrezze	1961	FB	D		66' 00"	17' 00"	5' 00"

C-10 — CLEVELAND TANKERS, INC., CLEVELAND, OH

Vessel Name	Year Built	Type of Ship	Type of Engine	Cargo Cap. or Gross*	Length	Beam	Depth or Draft*
Gemini	1978	TK	D	75,000	430' 00"	65' 00"	29' 04"
Saturn	1974	TK	D	48,000	384' 01"	54' 06"	25' 00"

C-11 — COASTWISE TRADING CO., EAST CHICAGO, IN

Vessel Name	Year Built	Type of Ship	Type of Engine	Cargo Cap. or Gross*	Length	Beam	Depth or Draft*
Great Lakes	1982	TK	B	75,000	414' 00"	60' 00"	30' 00"
(Amoco Great Lakes '82 - '85)							
Michigan	1982	TB	D	293*	107' 08"	34' 00"	16' 00"
(Amoco Michigan '82 - '85)							
(Overall Dimensions Together)					454' 00"	60' 00"	30' 00"

C-12 — CSX RAILROADS, PORT HURON, MI

Vessel Name	Year Built	Type of Ship	Type of Engine	Cargo Cap. or Gross*	Length	Beam	Depth or Draft*
C & O 452	1952	TB	D	239*	98' 00"	30' 00"	12' 00"
Pere Marquette 10	1945	TF	B	27 rail cars	400' 00"	53' 00"	22' 00"

(Both last operated October 7, 1994 - Both currently laid up in Port Huron, MI)

D-1 — DEAN CONSTRUCTION CO., BELLE RIVER, ON

Vessel Name	Year Built	Type of Ship	Type of Engine	Cargo Cap. or Gross*	Length	Beam	Depth or Draft*
Americo Dean	1956	TB	D	15*	45' 00"	15' 00"	5' 00"
Anne M. Dean	1981	TB	D	58*	50' 00"	19' 00"	5' 00"
Wayne Dean	1946	TB	D	10*	45' 00"	13' 00"	5' 00"
Neptune III	1939	TB	D	23*	53' 10"	15' 06"	5' 00"

D-2 — CITY OF DETROIT FIRE DEPT., DETROIT, MI

Vessel Name	Year Built	Type of Ship	Type of Engine	Cargo Cap. or Gross*	Length	Beam	Depth or Draft*
Curtiss Randolph	1979	FB	D		77' 10"	22' 02"	9' 02"

D-3 — DISSEN & JUHN CORP., MACEDON, NY

Vessel Name	Year Built	Type of Ship	Type of Engine	Cargo Cap. or Gross*	Length	Beam	Depth or Draft*
Constructor	1950	TB	D	14*	39' 00"	11' 00"	5' 00"
James W. Rickey	1935	TB	D	24*	46' 00"	14' 00"	7' 00"

D-4 — DOW CHEMICAL CO., MIDLAND, MI

Vessel Name	Year Built	Type of Ship	Type of Engine	Cargo Cap. or Gross*	Length	Beam	Depth or Draft*
DC 710	1969	TK	B	25,500	260' 00"	50' 00"	9' 00"

Rod Burdick

Self-unloader Joseph H. Frantz loads taconite tailings at Escanaba on 22 August, 1995.

Fleet No. and Name Vessel Name	Year Built	Type of Ship	Type of Engine	Cargo Cap. or Gross*	Length	Beam	Depth or Draft*

D-5 — DUROCHER DOCK & DREDGE, INC., CHEBOYGAN, MI

Vessel Name	Year Built	Type of Ship	Type of Engine	Cargo Cap. or Gross*	Length	Beam	Depth or Draft*
Betty D.	1953	TB	D	14*	40' 00"	13' 00"	6' 00"
Champion	1974	TB	D	125*	75' 00"	24' 00"	9' 06"
Ray Durocher	1943	TB	D	20*	45' 06"	12' 05"	7' 06"
General	1954	TB	D	119*	71' 00"	19' 06"	9' 06"
Meaghan Beth	1982	TB	D	94*	60' 00"	22' 00"	9' 00"
Nancy Anne	1969	TB	D	73*	60' 00"	20' 00"	6' 00"
Joe Van	1955	TB	D	32*	57' 09"	16' 06"	9' 00"
Witch	1950	TB	D	14*	30' 08"	9' 05"	6' 00"

Note: Various deck and crane barges are available.

E-1 — EAGLE MARINE TOWING, BURN HARBOR, IN

Vessel Name	Year Built	Type of Ship	Type of Engine	Cargo Cap. or Gross*	Length	Beam	Depth or Draft*
Blackie B.	1952	TB	D	146*	85' 00"	25' 00"	11' 00"
Frankie D.	1943	TB	D	196*	130' 00"	30' 00"	15' 01"

E-2 — EASTERN CANADA TOWING LTD., HALIFAX, NS

Vessel Name	Year Built	Type of Ship	Type of Engine	Cargo Cap. or Gross*	Length	Beam	Depth or Draft*
Point Carroll	1973	TB	D	366*	127' 00"	30' 05"	14' 05"
Point Chebucto	1992	TB	D	412*	110' 00"	33' 00"	17' 00"
Point Halifax	1986	TB	D	417*	110' 00"	36' 00"	19' 00"
Point Vibert	1961	TB	D	236*	96' 03"	28' 00"	14' 06"
Point Vigour	1962	TB	D	207*	98' 05"	26' 10"	13' 05"
Point Vim	1962	TB	D	207*	98' 05"	26' 10"	13' 05"
Pointe Aux Basques	1972	TB	D	396*	105' 00"	33' 06"	19' 06"
Pointe Comeau	1976	TB	D	391*	104' 00"	40' 00"	19' 00"
Pointe Sept Iles	1980	TB	D	424*	105' 00"	34' 06"	19' 06"

E-3 — ENERCHEM TRANSPORT, INC., MONTREAL, PQ

Vessel Name	Year Built	Type of Ship	Type of Engine	Cargo Cap. or Gross*	Length	Beam	Depth or Draft*
Enerchem Asphalt	1972	TK	D	133,858	414' 00"	52' 06"	36' 01"
(OT Marine '72 - '80, Asfamarine '80 - '88)							
Enerchem Catalyst	1972	TK	D	84,097	431' 00"	62' 04"	34' 05"
(Jon Ramsoy '72 - '74, Doan Transport '74 - '86)							
Enerchem Dolphin	1967	TK	D	72,077	411' 05"	55' 02"	27' 06"
(James Transport '67 - '86, Enerchem Travailleur '86 - '95)							
Enerchem Refiner	1969	TK	D	69,327	391' 00"	55' 00"	27' 06"
(Industrial Transport '69 - '86)							
Nordic Blossom	1981	TKD		151,580	505' 00"	74' 06"	45' 06"
(Nordic Sun '81 - '89, Nordic '89 - '94)							

E-4 — EDWIN M. ERICKSON, BAYFIELD, WI

Vessel Name	Year Built	Type of Ship	Type of Engine	Cargo Cap. or Gross*	Length	Beam	Depth or Draft*
Outer Island	1942	PK	D	300	112' 00"	32' 00"	8' 06"

E-5 — ERIE NAVIGATION CO., ERIE, PA

Vessel Name	Year Built	Type of Ship	Type of Engine	Cargo Cap. or Gross*	Length	Beam	Depth or Draft*
John R. Emery	1905	SC	D	490	140' 00"	33' 00"	14' 00"
(Trenton '05 - '28)							
Day Peckinpaugh	1921	CC	D	1,490	254' 00"	36' 00"	14' 00"
(Interwaterways Line Incorporated 101 '21 - '32, I.L.I. 101 '32 - '36, Richard J. Barnes '36 - '58)							
(Last operated September 9, 1994 — Currently laid up in Erie, PA)							

E-6 — ERIE SAND & GRAVEL CO., ERIE, PA

Vessel Name	Year Built	Type of Ship	Type of Engine	Cargo Cap. or Gross*	Length	Beam	Depth or Draft*
J. S. St. John	1945	SC	D	680	174' 00"	32' 02"	15' 00"
(USS YO-178 '45 - '51, Lake Edward '51 - '67)							

Fleet No. and Name / Vessel Name	Year Built	Type of Ship	Type of Engine	Cargo Cap. or Gross*	Length	Beam	Depth or Draft*
E-7 — ERIE SAND STEAMSHIP CO., ERIE, PA							
Richard Reiss	1943	SU	D	14,900	620' 06"	60' 03"	35' 00"
(Adirondack '43 - '43, Richard J. Reiss '43 - '86)							
E-8 — ESSROC CANADA, INC., TORONTO, ON							
Stephen B. Roman	1965	CC	D	7,600	488' 09"	56' 00"	35' 06"
(Fort William '65 - '83)							
Metis	1956	CC	B	5,800	331' 00"	43' 09"	26' 00"
(Last operated August 19, 1993 — Currently in use as a storage barge in Green Bay, WI)							
F-1 — FAUST CORP., GROSSE POINT FARMS, MI							
Comorant	1991	TB	D	10*	25' 02"	14' 00"	4' 06"
Linnhurst	1930	TB	D	11*	37' 06"	10' 06"	4' 08"
F-2 — FEDERAL TERMINALS LTD., QUEBEC CARTIER MINING CO., PORT CARTIER, PQ							
Brochu	1972	TB	D	390*	100' 00"	36' 00"	14' 06"
Vachon	1973	TB	D	390*	100' 00"	36' 00"	14' 06"
F-3 — FEDNAV INTERNATIONAL LTD., MONTREAL, PQ							
ARCTIC TRANSPORTATION							
Arctic Ivik		TB	D	1,565*			
Arctic Nutsukpok		TB	D	841*			
Arctic Surveyor		TB	D	736*			
Arctic Kibvayok		CB	B	9,500	312' 00"	111' 00"	
Arctic Kiggiak		CB	B	10,000	375' 00"	105' 00"	
BELCAN N.V.							
Cordillera	1984	BC	D	164,891	953' 07"	142' 02"	78' 05"
(Federal Hunter '84 - '95)							
Lake Erie	1980	BC	D	38,294	734' 02"	76' 08"	47' 05"
(Federal Ottawa '80 - '95)							
Lake Michigan	1981	BC	D	38,294	730' 00"	76' 08"	47' 05"
(Federal Maas '81 - '95)							
Lake Ontario	1980	BC	D	38,294	734' 02"	76' 08"	47' 05"
(Federal Danube '80 - '95)							
Lake Superior	1981	BC	D	38,294	734' 02"	76' 08"	47' 05"
(Federal Thames '81 - '95)							
Marine Hunter	1983	BC	D	164,891	874' 05"	142' 02"	78' 05"
(Federal Skenna '83 - '95)							
THE CARLTON STEAMSHIP CO., LTD							
Arctic Nanook		SB	D	520			
CIONA LTD.							
Georgios M.	1982	BC	D	140,784	879' 04"	141' 09"	77' 08"
(Orinoco '82 - '95)							
FEDERAL PACIFIC LTD.							
Federal Calliope	1978	BC	D	29,531	622' 07"	76' 05"	47' 05"
(Federal Saguenay '78 - '95)							
Federal Dora	1978	BC	D	29,531	622' 07"	76' 05"	47' 05"
(Federal St. Laurent '78 - '95)							
Federal Fuji	1986	BC	D	29,531	598' 00"	76' 00"	48' 00"
Federal Polaris	1985	BC	D	29,536	600' 00"	76' 00"	48' 00"
Federal St. Clair	1978	BC	D	38,450	734' 02"	76' 08"	47' 05"

Fleet No. and Name / Vessel Name	Year Built	Type of Ship	Type of Engine	Cargo Cap. or Gross*	Length	Beam	Depth or Draft*
Federal Schelde	1977	BC	D	38,568	734' 02"	76' 08"	47' 05"
OCEANEX LTD.							
ASL Sanderling		RR	D	14,689			
Cabot		RR	D	7,089			
Cicero		RR	D	7,132			
LONG TERM CHARTER							
APT Mariner	1979	BC	D	35,500	619' 00"	75' 10"	47' 07"
(Devonbrook '79 - '81)							
Federal Aalesund	1984	BC	D	30,674	590' 00"	75' 10"	50' 11"
(Fiona Mary '84 - '93)							
Federal Agno	1985	BC	D	29,643	600' 00"	75' 11"	48' 07"
(Federal Asahi '85 - '89)							
Federal Bergen	1984	BC	D	29,159	593' 00"	76' 00"	47' 00"
(High Peak '84 - '90, Federal Bergen '90 - '92, Thunder Bay '92 - '93)							
Federal Fraser	1983	BC	D	36,248	730' 00"	75' 09"	48' 00"
(Selkirk Settler '83 - '91, Federal St. Louis '91 - '91)							
Federal Inger	1977	BC	D	29,212	593' 00"	76' 00"	47' 00"
(Doric Javelin '77 - '89)							
Federal Kumano		BC	D	45,750			
Federal Mackenzie	1983	BC	D	36,248	730' 00"	75' 09"	48' 00"
(Canada Marquis '83 - '91, Federal Richelieu '91 - '91)							
Federal Manitou	1983	BC	D	28,192	585' 00"	75' 11"	48' 05"
(Kalliopi II '83 - '88, Cineraria '88 - '90, Consensus Star '90 - '91)							
Federal Matane	1984	BC	D	28,214	585' 00"	75' 10"	48' 05"
(Lake Shidaka '84 - '91, Consensus Atlantic '91 - '92)							
Federal Nord	1981	BC	D	29,466	591' 00"	76' 00"	47' 00"
(Violetta '81 - '86, Capetan Yiannis '86 - '88)							
Federal Oslo	1985	BC	D	29,462	601' 00"	76' 00"	48' 11"
(Paolo Pittaluga '85 - '91)							
Federal Pescadores		BC	D	40,864			
Federal Vibeke	1981	BC	D	30,900	618' 00"	76' 00"	47' 07"
(Nosira Lin '81 - '89, Dan Bauta '89 - '89, Kristianiafjord '89 - '93)							
Federal Vigra	1984	BC	D	30,674	590' 00"	75' 10"	50' 11"
(Mary Anne '84 - '93)							
Handy Mariner	1978	BC	D	31,200	619' 00"	75' 11"	47' 07"
(Durhambrook '78 - '80)							
Hope I	1982	BC	D	30,900	617' 00"	76' 00"	47' 07"
(Nosira Madeleine '82 - '89, Bella Dan '89 - '93)							
Island Gem	1984	BC	D	28,000	585' 00"	76' 02"	48' 05"
Island Skipper	1984	BC	D	28,031	585' 00"	76' 02"	48' 05"
Lake Carling	1993	BC	D	26,264	591' 00"	75' 09"	45' 07"
(Ziemia Cieszynska '93 - '93)							
Lake Champlain	1992	BC	D	26,264	591' 00"	75' 09"	45' 07"
(Ziemia Lodzka '92 - '92)							
Lake Charles	1990	BC	D	26,209	591' 00"	75' 09"	45' 07"
(Ziemia Gornoslaska '90 - '91)							
Mosdeep		BC	D	49,000			
Petka	1986	BC	D	35,500	729' 00"	75' 11"	48' 05"
Solta	1984	BC	D	29,643	625' 06"	75' 02"	50' 01"
NEW VESSELS							
Federal Baffin	1995	BC	D	44,000			
Federal Franklin	1995	BC	D	44,000			

Roger LeLievre

The 1927-built Kinsman Enterprise, upbound in the St. Mary's River, is every inch the classic, straight-deck bulk carrier.

Fleet No. and Name Vessel Name	Year Built	Type of Ship	Type of Engine	Cargo Cap. or Gross*	Length	Beam	Depth or Draft*
Federal St. Laurent	1996	BC	D	41,500	656' 00"	77' 00"	
New Building	1996	BC	D	41,500	656' 00"	77' 00"	
New Building	1996	BC	D	41,500	656' 00"	77' 00"	
New Building	1996	BC	D	54,000	623' 04"	100' 00"	
New Building	1997	BC	D	54,000	623' 04"	100' 00"	

F-4 — FERRIS MARINE CONTRACTING CORP., DETROIT, MI

Magnetic	1925	TB	D	30*	55' 00"	14' 00"	6' 06"
Norma B.	1940	TB	D	14*	43' 00"	15' 00"	4' 00"

F-5 — FRASER SHIPYARDS, INC., SUPERIOR, WI

Todd Fraser	1912	TB	D	71*	70' 00"	17' 00"	11' 00"
Su-Joy III	1941	TB	D	12*	40' 00"	10' 00"	5' 03"

G-1 — GAELIC TUG BOAT CO., GROSSE ILE, MI

Carolyn Hoey	1949	TB	D	146*	90' 00"	25' 00"	11' 00"
Patricia Hoey	1949	TB	D	146*	88' 06"	25' 00"	11' 00"
Kaw	1943	TB	D	346*	110' 00"	26' 05"	11' 11"
Shannon	1944	TB	D	145*	101' 00"	26' 00"	13' 00"
G.T.B. 1	1956	DB	B	2,500	248' 00"	43' 00"	12' 00"
L.S.C. 236	1946	TK	B	10,000	195' 00"	35' 00"	10' 06"
Marysville	1973	TK	B	16,000	200' 00"	50' 00"	10' 06"

G-2 — GALLAGHER MARINE CONSTRUCTION CO., INC., ESCANABA, MI

Bee Jay	1939	TB	D	19*	45' 00"	13' 00"	7' 00"

G-3 — HARRY GAMBLE SHIPYARDS, PORT DOVER, ON

Husky 120	1931	TK	D	1,649	139' 00"	29' 00"	9' 00"

(John George '31 - '32, Britamette '32 - '56)
(Last operated in 1968 — Currently laid up in Port Dover, ON)

H. A. Smith	1944	TB	D	24*	55' 00"	16' 00"	5' 06"

G-4 — EDWARD E. GILLEN CO., MILWAUKEE, WI

Andrew J.	1950	TB	D	25*	47' 00"	15' 07"	8' 00"
Edith J.	1962	TB	D	19*	45' 03"	13' 00"	8' 00"
Edward E. Gillen III	1988	TB	D	95*	75' 00"	26' 00"	9' 06"

Note: Various deck and crane barges are available.

G-5 — GILLESPIE OIL & TRANSIT, INC., ST. JAMES, MI

American Girl	1922	PK	D	40	64' 00"	14' 00"	8' 03"
Oil Queen	1949	TK	B	620	65' 00"	16' 00"	6' 00"

G-6 — GODERICH ELEVATORS LTD., GODERICH, ON

Willowglen	1943	BC	B	16,300	620' 06"	60' 00"	35' 00"

(Lehigh '43 - '81, Joseph X. Robert '81 - '82)
(Last operated December 21, 1992 — Currently in use as a storage barge in Goderich, ON)

G-7 — GORDON WELDING, SARNIA, ON

W. C. Harms	1949	TB	D	147*	78' 00"	24' 00"	9' 08"

G-8 — GRAVEL & LAKE SERVICES LTD., THUNDER BAY, ON

George N. Carleton	1943	TB	D	97*	82' 00"	21' 00"	11' 00"

Fleet No. and Name Vessel Name	Year Built	Type of Ship	Type of Engine	Cargo Cap. or Gross*	Length	Beam	Depth or Draft*
Donald Mac	1914	TB	D	69*	71' 00"	17' 00"	10' 00"
Peninsula	1944	TB	D	261*	104' 06"	26' 06"	12' 06"
F. A. Johnson	1953	TB	D	439*	150' 00"	32' 00"	10' 00"
R. G. Cassidy	1952	TB	B	286*	115' 01"	30' 00"	9' 08"
Robert John	1945	TB	D	98*	82' 00"	21' 00"	11' 00"
Wolf River	1956	BC	B	5,880	349' 00"	43' 06"	25' 06"

(Tecumseh '56 - '67, New York News '67 - '86, Stella Desgagnes '86 - '94, Beam Beginner '94 - '95)

G-9 — GREAT LAKES DREDGE & DOCK CO., OAK BROOK, IL

Douglas B. Mackie	1978	TB	D	98*	72' 00"	26' 00"	7' 06"

G-10 — GREAT LAKES INT. TOWING & SALVAGE, INC., BURLINGTON, ON

Petite Forte	1969	TB	D	368*	127' 00"	32' 00"	14' 06"
R. & L. No. 1	1979	TB	D	145*	91' 00"	26' 00"	8' 06"

G-11 — GREAT LAKES MARITIME ACADEMY, TRAVERSE CITY, MI

Anchor Bay	1953	TV	D	23*	44' 00"	11' 06"	7' 00"
Northwestern	1960	TV	D	77*	79' 00"	9' 00"	8' 00"
Wolverine	1954	TV	D	12*	40' 00"	10' 00"	3' 00"
Barge		TV	B		80' 00"	20' 00"	7' 00"

G-12 — GREAT LAKES SHIPWRECK HISTORICAL SOCIETY, SAULT STE. MARIE, MI

Antiquarian		RV	D		40' 00"	12' 00"	4' 00"
David Boyd		RV	D				

G-13 — GREAT LAKES TOWING CO., CLEVELAND, OH

Alabama	1957	TB	D	98*	81' 00"	21' 03"	12' 05"
Alaska	1912	TB	D	36*	74' 00"	19' 06"	12' 00"
Arizona	1955	TB	D	98*	81' 00"	21' 03"	12' 05"
Arkansas	1949	TB	D	98*	81' 00"	21' 03"	12' 05"
California	1951	TB	D	98*	81' 00"	21' 03"	12' 05"
Colorado	1954	TB	D	98*	81' 00"	21' 03"	12' 05"
Connecticut	1958	TB	D	98*	81' 00"	21' 03"	12' 05"
Delaware	1951	TB	D	98*	81' 00"	21' 03"	12' 05"
El Lobo Grande II	1978	TB	D	199*	136' 02"	36' 05"	18' 00"
Florida	1955	TB	D	98*	81' 00"	21' 03"	12' 05"
Georgia	1952	TB	D	199*	110' 00"	22' 00"	12' 00"
Idaho	1957	TB	D	98*	81' 00"	21' 03"	12' 05"
Illinois	1949	TB	D	98*	81' 00"	21' 03"	12' 05"
Indiana	1958	TB	D	98*	81' 00"	21' 03"	12' 05"
Iowa	1951	TB	D	98*	81' 00"	21' 03"	12' 05"
Kansas	1958	TB	D	98*	81' 00"	21' 03"	12' 05"
Kentucky	1959	TB	D	98*	81' 00"	21' 03"	12' 05"
Louisiana	1950	TB	D	98*	81' 00"	21' 03"	12' 05"
Maine	1951	TB	D	98*	81' 00"	21' 03"	12' 05"
Maryland	1952	TB	D	98*	81' 00"	21' 03"	12' 05"
Massachusetts	1959	TB	D	98*	81' 00"	21' 03"	12' 05"
Michigan	1915	TB	D	98*	81' 00"	21' 03"	12' 05"
Minnesota	1960	TB	D	98*	81' 00"	21' 03"	12' 05"
Mississippi	1957	TB	D	98*	81' 00"	21' 03"	12' 05"
Missouri	1927	TB	D	101*	94' 00"	26' 00"	13' 00"
Montana	1956	TB	D	98*	81' 00"	21' 03"	12' 05"

Fleet No. and Name Vessel Name	Year Built	Type of Ship	Type of Engine	Cargo Cap. or Gross*	Length	Beam	Depth or Draft*
Nebraska	1955	TB	D	98*	84' 04"	21' 03"	12' 05"
Nevada	1959	TB	D	98*	81' 00"	21' 03"	12' 05"
New Hampshire	1931	TB	D	149*	85' 00"	25' 00"	11' 00"
New Jersey	1959	TB	D	98*	81' 00"	21' 03"	12' 05"
New Mexico	1957	TB	D	98*	81' 00"	21' 03"	12' 05"
New York	1960	TB	D	98*	81' 00"	21' 03"	12' 05"
North Carolina	1952	TB	D	145*	95' 06"	25' 00"	12' 00"
North Dakota	1949	TB	D	98*	81' 00"	21' 03"	12' 05"
Ohio	1954	TB	D	194*	118' 00"	26' 00"	13' 06"
Oklahoma	1951	TB	D	98*	81' 00"	21' 03"	12' 05"
Oregon	1952	TB	D	149*	89' 00"	25' 00"	12' 00"
Pennsylvania	1960	TB	D	98*	81' 00"	21' 03"	12' 05"
Rhode Island	1958	TB	D	98*	81' 00"	21' 03"	12' 05"
South Carolina	1948	TB	D	102*	85' 00"	22' 06"	11' 00"
Superior	1953	TB	D	147*	82' 00"	22' 00"	12' 05"
Tennessee	1960	TB	D	98*	81' 00"	21' 03"	12' 05"
Texas	1951	TB	D	98*	81' 00"	21' 03"	12' 05"
Utah	1950	TB	D	98*	81' 00"	21' 03"	12' 05"
Vermont	1949	TB	D	98*	81' 00"	21' 03"	12' 05"
Virginia	1951	TB	D	98*	81' 00"	21' 03"	12' 05"
Washington	1951	TB	D	98*	81' 00"	21' 03"	12' 05"
Wisconsin	1950	TB	D	106*	90' 03"	22' 05"	13' 05"
Wyoming	1953	TB	D	98*	84' 04"	21' 03"	12' 05"

H-1 — HALRON OIL CO., INC., GREEN BAY, WI

Mr. Micky	1940	TK	B	10,500	195' 00"	35' 00"	10' 00"

H-2 — HAMILTON HARBOUR COMMISSIONERS, HAMILTON, ON

Judge McCombs	1948	TB	D	10*	36' 00"	10' 03"	4' 00"

H-3 — HANNAH MARINE CORP., LEMONT, IL

Daryl C. Hannah	1956	TB	D	268*	102' 00"	28' 00"	8' 00"
Donald C. Hannah	1962	TB	D	191*	91' 00"	29' 00"	11' 06"
Hannah D. Hannah	1955	TB	D	134*	86' 00"	24' 00"	10' 00"
James A. Hannah	1945	TB	D	593*	149' 00"	33' 00"	16' 00"
Kristen Lee Hannah	1945	TB	D	602*	149' 00"	33' 00"	16' 00"
Mark Hannah	1969	TB	D	191*	127' 05"	32' 01"	14' 03"
Mary E. Hannah	1945	TB	D	612*	149' 00"	33' 00"	16' 00"
Mary Page Hannah	1972	TB	D	99*	59' 08"	24' 01"	10' 03"
Peggy D. Hannah	1920	TB	D	145*	108' 00"	25' 00"	14' 00"
Susan W. Hannah	1977	TB	D	174*	121' 06"	34' 06"	18' 02"
Hannah 1801	1967	TK	B	18,550	240' 00"	50' 00"	12' 00"
Hannah 1802	1967	TK	B	18,550	240' 00"	50' 00"	12' 00"
Hannah 2801	1980	TK	B	28,665	275' 00"	54' 00"	17' 06"
Hannah 2901	1962	TK	B	17,400	264' 00"	52' 06"	12' 06"
Hannah 2902	1962	TK	B	17,360	264' 00"	52' 06"	12' 06"
Hannah 2903	1962	TK	B	17,350	264' 00"	52' 06"	12' 06"
Hannah 3601	1972	TK	B	35,360	290' 00"	60' 00"	18' 03"
Hannah 5101	1978	TK	B	49,660	360' 00"	60' 00"	22' 06"
No. 25	1949	TK	B	19,500	254' 00"	54' 00"	11' 00"
No. 26	1949	TK	B	19,500	254' 00"	54' 00"	11' 00"

Fleet No. and Name Vessel Name	Year Built	Type of Ship	Type of Engine	Cargo Cap. or Gross*	Length	Beam	Depth or Draft*
No. 28	1957	TK	B	20,725	240' 00"	50' 00"	12' 06"
No. 29	1952	TK	B	22,000	254' 00"	54' 00"	11' 06"

H-4 — HOLLY MARINE TOWING, CHICAGO, IL

Vessel Name	Year Built	Type of Ship	Type of Engine	Cargo Cap. or Gross*	Length	Beam	Depth or Draft*
Holly Ann	1926	TB	D	220*	108' 00"	26' 06"	15' 00"
Katie Ann	1924	TB	D	99*	85' 00"	21' 06"	10' 09"
Margaret Ann	1954	TB	D	131*	82' 00"	24' 06"	11' 06"
Laura Lynn	1950	TB	D	146*	82' 00"	25' 00"	10' 07"

I-1 — IMPERIAL OIL LTD., DARTMOUTH, NS

Vessel Name	Year Built	Type of Ship	Type of Engine	Cargo Cap. or Gross*	Length	Beam	Depth or Draft*
Imperial Acadia	1966	TK	D	84,000	440' 00"	60' 00"	31' 00"
Imperial Bedford	1969	TK	D	118,000	485' 05"	70' 02"	33' 03"
Imperial Dartmouth	1970	TK	D	15,265	205' 06"	40' 00"	16' 00"
Imperial Lachine	1963	TK	D	9,385	175' 00"	36' 00"	14' 00"
Imperial St. Clair	1974	TK	D	106,000	435' 00"	74' 00"	32' 00"

I-2 - INLAND LAKES MANAGEMENT / TRANSPORTATION, INC., ALPENA, MI

Vessel Name	Year Built	Type of Ship	Type of Engine	Cargo Cap. or Gross*	Length	Beam	Depth or Draft*
Alpena	1942	CC	T	15,550	519' 06"	67' 00"	35' 00"
(Leon Fraser '42 - '91)							
S. T. Crapo	1927	CC	R	8,900	402' 06"	60' 03"	29' 00"
E. M. Ford	1898	CC	Q	7,100	428' 00"	50' 00"	28' 00"
(Presque Isle 1898 - '56)							
J. B. Ford	1904	CC	R	8,000	440' 00"	50' 00"	28' 00"
(Edwin F. Holmes '04 - '16, E. C. Collins '16 - '59)							

(Last operated November 15, 1985 — Currently in use as a cement storage / transfer vessel in South Chicago, IL)

Vessel Name	Year Built	Type of Ship	Type of Engine	Cargo Cap. or Gross*	Length	Beam	Depth or Draft*
Lewis G. Harriman	1923	CC	B	5,500	350' 00"	55' 00"	28' 00"
(John W. Boardman '23 - '65)							

(Last operated April 20, 1980 — Currently in use as a transfer barge in Milwaukee, WI)

Vessel Name	Year Built	Type of Ship	Type of Engine	Cargo Cap. or Gross*	Length	Beam	Depth or Draft*
J. A. W. Iglehart	1936	CC	T	12,500	501' 06"	68' 03"	37' 00"
(Pan Amoco '36 - '55, Amoco '55 - '60, H. R. Schemn '60 - '65)							
Paul H. Townsend	1945	CC	D	8,400	447' 00"	50' 00"	29' 00"
(Hickory Coll '45 - '46, Coastal Delegate '46 - '52)							

I-3 — INLAND STEEL CO., EAST CHICAGO, IN

Vessel Name	Year Built	Type of Ship	Type of Engine	Cargo Cap. or Gross*	Length	Beam	Depth or Draft*
Joseph L. Block	1976	SU	D	37,200	728' 00"	78' 00"	45' 00"
Edward L. Ryerson	1960	BC	T	27,500	730' 00"	75' 00"	39' 00"

(Last operated January 24, 1994 — Currently laid up in Sturgeon Bay, WI)

Vessel Name	Year Built	Type of Ship	Type of Engine	Cargo Cap. or Gross*	Length	Beam	Depth or Draft*
Wilfred Sykes	1949	SU	D	21,500	678' 00"	70' 00"	37' 00"

AMERICAN STEAMSHIP CO. — CHARTERED

Vessel Name	Year Built	Type of Ship	Type of Engine	Cargo Cap. or Gross*	Length	Beam	Depth or Draft*
Adam E. Cornelius	1973	SU	D	28,200	680' 00"	78' 00"	42' 00"
(Roger M. Kyes '73 - '89)							

I-4 — THE INTERLAKE STEAMSHIP CO., CLEVELAND, OH

Vessel Name	Year Built	Type of Ship	Type of Engine	Cargo Cap. or Gross*	Length	Beam	Depth or Draft*
James R. Barker	1976	SU	D	63,300	1,004' 00"	105' 00"	50' 00"
Charles M. Beeghly	1959	SU	T	31,000	806' 00"	75' 00"	37' 06"
(Shenango II '59 - '67)							
Elton Hoyt 2nd	1952	SU	T	22,300	698' 00"	70' 00"	37' 00"
Herbert C. Jackson	1959	SU	T	24,800	690' 00"	75' 00"	37' 06"
J. L. Mauthe	1953	BC	T	21,400	647' 00"	70' 00"	36' 00"

(Last operated July 5, 1993 — Currently laid up in Superior, WI)

Vessel Name	Year Built	Type of Ship	Type of Engine	Cargo Cap. or Gross*	Length	Beam	Depth or Draft*
Mesabi Miner	1977	SU	D	63,300	1,004' 00"	105' 00"	50' 00"

Fleet No. and Name Vessel Name	Year Built	Type of Ship	Type of Engine	Cargo Cap. or Gross*	Length	Beam	Depth or Draft*
George A. Stinson	1978	SU	D	59,700	1,004' 00"	105' 00"	50' 00"
Paul R. Tregurtha	1981	SU	D	68,000	1,013' 06"	105' 00"	56' 00"

(William J. DeLancey '81 - '90)

LAKES SHIPPING CO.

Kaye E. Barker	1952	SU	T	25,900	767' 00"	70' 00"	36' 00"

(Edward B. Greene '52 - '85, Benson Ford '85 - '89)

John Sherwin	1958	BC	T	31,500	806' 00"	75' 00"	37' 06"

(Last operated November 16, 1981 — Currently laid up in Superior, WI)

Lee A. Tregurtha	1942	SU	T	29,300	826' 00"	75' 00"	39' 00"

(Samoset '42 - '42, Chiwawa '42 - '61, Walter A. Sterling '61 - '85, William Clay Ford '85 - '89)

J-1 — JULIO CONTRACTING CO., HANCOCK, MI

Julio	1941	TB	D	84*	71' 00"	18' 00"	9' 06"
Winnebago	1945	TB	D	14*	40' 00"	10' 02"	4' 06"

K-1 — KADINGER MARINE SERVICE, INC., MILWAUKEE, WI

David Kadinger Jr.	1969	TB	D	98*	65' 06"	22' 00"	8' 06"
Ruffy J. Kadinger	1981	TB	D	74*	55' 00"	23' 00"	7' 02"

K-2 — KELLSTONE, INC., CLEVELAND, OH

Frank Palladino Jr.	1980	TB	D	89*	100' 00"	32' 00"	13' 00"
Benjamin Ridgeway	1969	TB	D	51*	53' 00"	18' 05"	7' 05"
Kellstone I	1957	DB	B	9,000	396' 00"	71' 00"	22' 06"

K-3 — KENT LINE LTD., SAINT JOHN, NB

Irving Arctic	1974	TK	D	146,048	632' 06"	90' 07"	48' 05"
Irving Canada	1981	TK	D	148,238	632' 06"	90' 07"	48' 05"
Irving Eskimo	1980	TK	D	147,118	632' 06"	90' 07"	48' 05"
Irving Ocean	1981	TK	D	148,238	632' 06"	90' 07"	48' 05"
Irving Timber	1978	RR	D	7,087	415' 00"	66' 03"	38' 05"
Wellington Kent	1980	TK	D	48,741	436' 05"	67' 06"	30' 06"

(Irving Nordic '80 - '94)

K-4 — KINDRA LAKE TOWING, CHICAGO, IL

Buckley	1958	TB	D	94*	95' 00"	26' 00"	11' 00"
Morgan	1974	TB	D	134*	90' 00"	30' 00"	10' 06"
Old Mission	1944	TB	D	94*	85' 00"	23' 00"	10' 04"

K-5 — KING CONSTRUCTION CO., HOLLAND, MI

Barry J	1943	TB	D	42*	46' 00"	13' 00"	7' 00"
Carol Ann	1981	TB	D	67*	68' 00"	24' 00"	5' 00"
John Henry	1989	TB	D	66*	70' 00"	20' 06"	9' 07"
Julie Dee	1903	TB	D	59*	63' 03"	17' 05"	9' 00"
Ludington	1979	TB	D	67*	69' 03"	17' 05"	11' 05"
Miss Edna	1935	TB	D	29*	36' 08"	11' 02"	4' 08"
Muskegon	1973	TB	D	138*	75' 00"	24' 00"	11' 06"

K-6 — KINSMAN LINES, INC., CLEVELAND, OH

Kinsman Enterprise	1927	BC	T	16,000	631' 00"	65' 00"	33' 00"

(Harry Coulby '27 - '89)

Kinsman Independent	1952	BC	T	18,800	642' 03"	67' 00"	35' 00"

(Charles L. Hutchinson '52 - '62, Ernest R. Breech '62 - '88)

Jim Hoffman

ULS Corporation's Gordon C. Leitch, the former Ralph Misener, upbound in the Maumee River at Toledo.

Fleet No. and Name Vessel Name	Year Built	Type of Ship	Type of Engine	Cargo Cap. or Gross*	Length	Beam	Depth or Draft*
K-7 — KUHLMAN CORP., TOLEDO, OH							
Sand Pebble	1969	TB	D	30*	46' 00"	15' 00"	7' 07"
L-1 — LAKE MICHIGAN CONTRACTORS, INC., HOLLAND, MI							
Capt. Barnaby	1956	TB	D	146*	94' 00"	27' 00"	11' 09"
Curly B.	1965	TB	D	131*	84' 00"	26' 00"	9' 02"
G. W. Falcon	1936	TB	D	22*	49' 07"	13' 08"	6' 02"
James Harris	1943	TB	D	18*	41' 09"	12' 05"	5' 07"
Art Lapish	1954	TB	D	15*	44' 03"	12' 08"	5' 04"

Note: Various deck and crane barges are available.

Fleet No. and Name Vessel Name	Year Built	Type of Ship	Type of Engine	Cargo Cap. or Gross*	Length	Beam	Depth or Draft*
L-2 — LAKE MICHIGAN HARDWARE CO., LELAND, MI							
Glen Shore	1957	PK	D	105	68' 00"	21' 00"	6' 00"
L-3 — LAKE TOWING, INC., AVON, OH							
Jiggs	1911	TB	D	45*	61' 00"	16' 00"	8' 00"
Johnson	1976	TB	D	287*	140' 06"	40' 00"	15' 06"
Johnson II	1975	TB	D	311*	194' 00"	40' 00"	17' 00"
2361	1967	BC	B	3,600	236' 00"	50' 00"	15' 10"
3403	1963	SU	B	9,500	340' 00"	62' 06"	25 '04"
L-4 — LOWER LAKES TOWING LTD., PORT DOVER, ON							
Cuyahoga	1943	SU	L	15,675	620' 00"	60' 00"	35' 00"
(J. Burton Ayers '43 - '95)							
Thomas A. Payette	1948	TB	D	123*	86' 00"	21' 00"	10' 00"
L-5 — LUEDTKE ENGINEERING CO., FRANKFORT, MI							
Gretchen B.	1943	TB	D	18*	45' 00"	12' 03"	6' 00"
Alan K. Luedtke	1944	TB	D	163*	86' 00"	23' 00"	10' 00"
Chris E. Luedtke	1936	TB	D	18*	45' 00"	12' 03"	6' 00"
Erich R. Luedtke	1939	TB	D	18*	45' 00"	12' 03"	6' 00"
Karl E. Luedtke	1928	TB	D	32*	59' 03"	14' 09"	8' 00"
Kurt Luedtke	1956	TB	D	95*	72' 00"	22' 06"	7' 06"
Kurt R. Luedtke	1928	TB	D	61*	63' 00"	16' 07"	7' 07"
Paul L. Luedtke	1935	TB	D	18*	42' 06"	11' 09"	6' 09"
M-1 — MACDONALD MARINE LTD., GODERICH, ON							
Debbie Lyn	1950	TB	D	10*	45' 00"	14' 00"	10' 00"
Donald Bert	1953	TB	D	11*	45' 00"	14' 00"	10' 00"
Ian Mac	1955	TB	D	12*	45' 00"	14' 00"	10' 00"
M-2 — MALCOM MARINE, ST. CLAIR, MI							
Manitou	1943	TB	D	491*	110' 00"	27' 00"	11' 00"
Tug Malcom	1944	TB	D	508*	143' 00"	33' 09"	14' 06"
M-3 — DAVID MALLOCH, SCUDDER, ON							
Cemba	1960	TK	D	944	50' 00"	15' 06"	7' 06"
M-4 — MANSON CONSTRUCTION CO., INC., NORTH TONAWANDA, NY							
Burro	1965	TB	D	19*	36' 00"	13' 03"	5' 01"
J. G. II	1944	TB	D	16*	42' 03"	13' 00"	5' 06"
Marcey	1966	TB	D	22*	42' 00"	12' 06"	6' 10"

Fleet No. and Name Vessel Name	Year Built	Type of Ship	Type of Engine	Cargo Cap. or Gross*	Length	Beam	Depth or Draft*
M-5 — MARINE MANAGEMENT, INC., BRUSSELS, WI							
Nathan S.	1954	TB	D	76*	66' 00"	19' 00"	9' 00"
M-6 — MARINE FUELING CO., SUPERIOR, WI							
Reiss Marine	1978	TK	D	8,000	149' 06"	39' 06"	14' 08'
M-7 — MARINE TECH OF DULUTH, INC., DULUTH, MN							
Howard T. Hagen	1910	TB	D	51*	64' 00"	16' 09"	8' 06"
Jana	1954	TB	D	15*	49' 06"	13' 00"	7' 00"
Jason	1945	TB	D	21*	48' 00"	12' 01"	7' 00"
M-8 — MARITIME INVESTING LLC., NAPERVILLE, IL							
Manitowoc	1926	TF	B	27 rail cars	371' 03"	67' 03"	22' 06"
Roanoke	1930	TF	B	30 rail cars	381' 06"	58' 03"	22' 06"
(City of Flint 32 '30 - '70)							
Windsor	1930	TF	B	28 rail cars	370' 03"	65' 09"	22' 06"
(All last operated May 1, 1994 — All currently laid up in Toledo, OH)							
M-9 — MCALLISTER TOWING & SALVAGE, INC., MONTREAL, PQ							
Felicia	1923	TB	D	183*	91' 02"	24' 01"	12' 00"
Cathy McAllister	1954	TB	D	225*	101' 09"	26' 01"	13' 05"
Daniel McAllister	1907	TB	D	286*	115' 00"	23' 04"	14' 00"
Helen M. McAllister	1959	TB	D	152*	105' 00"	23' 04"	14' 00"
Salvage Monarch	1959	TB	D	219*	97' 09"	28' 00"	14' 06"
Sinmac	1959	TB	D	224*	90' 00"	26' 00"	13' 00"
Omni Sorel	1962	TB	D	80*	72' 00"	19' 00"	12' 00"
M-10 — McASPHALT INDUSTRIES LTD., SCARBOROUGH, ON							
McAsphalt 401	1966	TK	B	43,000	300' 00"	60' 00"	23' 00"
M-11 — MCKEIL MARINE LTD., HAMILTON, ON							
D. C. Everest	1953	CS	D	2,860	259' 00"	43' 06"	21' 00"
(D. C. Everest '53 - '81, Condarrell '81 - '88)							
Atomic	1945	TB	D	96*	82' 00"	20' 00"	10' 00"
Beaver D.	1955	TB	D	15*	36' 02"	14' 09"	4' 04"
Billie M.	1897	TB	D	34*	58' 00"	16' 00"	5' 06"
Carolyn Jo	1941	TB	D	60*	62' 00"	17' 00"	7' 08"
Dufresne	1944	TB	D	30*	58' 08"	14' 08"	5' 08"
Glenbrook	1944	TB	D	91*	81' 00"	21' 00"	9' 00"
Glenevis	1944	TB	D	91*	81' 00"	21' 00"	9' 00"
Kate B.	1950	TB	D	12*	46' 00"	12' 00"	3' 00"
Lac Como	1943	TB	D	64*	60' 09"	16' 06"	7' 09"
Lac Erie	1944	TB	D	65*	60' 09"	16' 06"	7' 09"
Lac Manitoba	1944	TB	D	65*	60' 09"	16' 06"	7' 09"
Lac Vancouver	1943	TB	D	65*	60' 09"	16' 06"	7' 09"
Evans B. McKeil	1936	TB	D	284*	110' 00"	25' 06"	11' 06"
Jerry Newberry	1957	TB	D	244*	98' 00"	28' 00"	14' 00"
Offshore Supplier	1979	TB	D	127*	92' 00"	25' 00"	10' 00"
Paul E. No. 1	1945	TB	D	97*	80' 00"	20' 00"	9' 06"
John Spence	1972	TB	D	719*	171' 00"	38' 00"	16' 00"
Stormont	1953	TB	D	108*	74' 00"	20' 00"	8' 00"

Fleet No. and Name Vessel Name	Year Built	Type of Ship	Type of Engine	Cargo Cap. or Gross*	Length	Beam	Depth or Draft*
Otis Wack	1950	TB	D	163*	102' 06"	26' 01"	13' 06"
Willmac	1959	TB	D	16*	40' 00"	13' 00"	5' 08"
Sillery	1963	ER	D	9,384	175' 00"	36' 00"	14' 00"
S.M.T.B. No. 7	1969	ER	B	7,502	150' 00"	33' 00"	14' 00"
Dover Light	1967	TK	B	7,870	146' 05"	35' 05"	14' 01"
Salty Dog 1	1945	TK	B	88,735	313' 00"	68' 03"	26' 07"
Toledo	1962	TK	B	6,388	135' 00"	34' 00"	9' 00"
McAllister 252	1969	DB	B	2,636*	250' 00"	76' 01"	16' 01"
Niagara II	1930	SC	B	600	182' 06"	35' 03"	13' 00"

(Rideaulite '30 - '47, Imperial Lachine '47 - '54, Niagara '54 - '69, W. M. Edington '69 - '84)

Note: Various deck and crane barges are available.

M-12 — MCMULLEN & PITZ CONSTRUCTION CO., MANITOWOC, WI

Dauntless	1937	TB	D	25*	52' 06"	15' 06"	5' 03"

M-13 — MEDUSA CEMENT CO., CLEVELAND, OH

Medusa Challenger	1906	CC	S	10,250	552' 01"	56' 00"	31' 00"

(William P Snyder '06 - '26, Elton Hoyt II '26 - '52, Alex D. Chisholm '52 - '66)

Medusa Conquest	1937	CC	B	8,500	437' 06"	55' 00"	28' 00"

(Red Crown '37 - '62, Amoco Indiana '62 - '87)

CTC #1	1943	CC	B	16,300	620' 06"	60' 00"	35' 00"

(Frank Purnell '43 - '66, Steelton '66 - '78, Hull No. 3 '78 - '79, Pioneer '79 - '80)
(Last operated November 12, 1981 — Currently in use as a cement storage / transfer barge in South Chicago, IL)

M-14 — MERCE TRANSPORTATION CO., SYLVANIA, OH

Triton	1941	TB	D	196*	131' 00"	30' 00"	17' 05"

M-15 — MICHIGAN DEPT. OF NATURAL RESOURCES, LANSING, MI

Channel Cat		RV	D		46' 00"	13' 06"	4' 00"
Chinook		RV	D		50' 00"	12' 00"	5' 00"
Judy		RV	D		40' 00"	12' 00"	3' 06"
Steelhead		RV	D		63' 00"	16' 04"	6' 06"

M-16 — UNIVERSITY OF MICHIGAN - GREAT LAKES & AQUATIC SERVICES, ANN ARBOR, MI

Laurentian		RV	D		80' 00"	21' 06"	8' 09"

M-17 — CITY OF MILWAUKEE FIRE DEPT., MILWAUKEE, WI

Amphibious		FB	D		35' 00"		

M-18 — MONTREAL MARINE TUG, INC., MONTREAL, PQ

Escorte	1964	TB	D		79' 00"	23' 00"	9' 00"

M-19 — MORTON SALT CO., CHICAGO, IL

Morton Salt 74	1974	DB	B	2,101	195' 00"	35' 00"	12' 00"

N-1 — NELSON CONSTRUCTION CO., LAPOINTE, WI

Eclipse	1937	TB	D	23*	47' 00"	13' 00"	6' 00"
No. 66-4	1960	DB	B	155	80' 00"	30' 00"	8' 00"

Saltie Turid Knutsen and laker Middletown pass in the South Channel off Ha

...me	Year Built	Type of Ship	Type of Engine	Cargo Cap. or Gross*	Length	Beam	Depth or Draft*

...CHOLSON TERMINAL & DOCK CO., RIVER ROUGE, MI

Name	Year Built	Type of Ship	Type of Engine	Cargo Cap. or Gross*	Length	Beam	Depth or Draft*
E. Jackson	1956	TB	D	12*	35' 00"	10' 06"	5' 01"
	1904	TF	B	22 rail cars	308' 00"	76' 09"	19' 06"

— OGLEBAY NORTON CO., CLEVELAND, OH

Name	Year Built	Type of Ship	Type of Engine	Cargo Cap. or Gross*	Length	Beam	Depth or Draft*
...mco	1953	SU	T	25,500	767' 00"	70' 00"	36' 00"
...uckeye	1952	SU	T	22,300	698' 00"	70' 00"	37' 00"
(Sparrows Point '52 - '91)							
Courtney Burton	1953	SU	T	22,300	690' 00"	70' 00"	37' 00"
(Ernest T. Weir '53 - '78)							
Columbia Star	1981	SU	D	78,850	1,000' 00"	105' 00"	56' 00"
Joseph H. Frantz	1925	SU	D	13,600	618' 00"	62' 00"	32' 00"
Middletown	1943	SU	T	26,300	730' 00"	75' 00"	39' 03"
(Marquette '43 - '43, USS Neshanic '43 - '47, Gulfoil '47 - '61, Pioneer Challenger '61 - '62)							
David Z. Norton	1973	SU	D	19,650	630' 00"	68' 00"	36' 11"
(William R. Roesch '73 - '95)							
Oglebay Norton	1978	SU	D	78,850	1,000' 00"	105' 00"	56' 00"
(Lewis Wilson Foy '78 - '91)							
Earl W. Oglebay	1973	SU	D	19,650	630' 00"	68' 00"	36' 11"
(Paul Thayer '73 - '95)							
Reserve	1953	SU	T	25,500	767' 00"	70' 00"	36' 00"
Fred R. White Jr.	1979	SU	D	23,800	636' 00"	68' 00"	40' 00"
Wolverine	1974	SU	D	19,650	630' 00"	68' 00"	36' 11"

O-2 — OSBORNE MATERIALS CO., MENTOR, OH

Name	Year Built	Type of Ship	Type of Engine	Cargo Cap. or Gross*	Length	Beam	Depth or Draft*
Emmet J. Carey	1948	SC	D	900	114' 00"	23' 00"	11' 00"
(Beatrice Ottinger '48 - '63, James B. Lyons '63 - '88)							
F. M. Osborne	1910	SC	D	500	150' 00"	29' 00"	11' 03"
(Grand Island '10 - '58, Lesco '58 - '75)							

P-1 — P.& H. SHIPPING, DIV. OF PARRISH & HEIMBECKER LTD., MISSISSAUGA, ON

Name	Year Built	Type of Ship	Type of Engine	Cargo Cap. or Gross*	Length	Beam	Depth or Draft*
Mapleglen	1960	BC	T	26,100	715' 03"	75' 00"	37' 09"
(Carol Lake '60 - '87, Algocape '87 - '94)							
Oakglen	1954	BC	T	22,950	714' 06"	70' 03"	37' 03"
(T. R. McLagan '54 - '90)							

P-2 — N. M. PATERSON & SONS LTD., THUNDER BAY, ON

Name	Year Built	Type of Ship	Type of Engine	Cargo Cap. or Gross*	Length	Beam	Depth or Draft*
Cartierdoc	1959	BC	D	29,100	730' 00"	75' 09"	40' 02"
(Ems Ore '59 - '76, Montcliffe Hall '76 - '88)							
Comeaudoc	1960	BC	D	26,750	730' 00"	75' 06"	37' 09"
(Murray Bay '60 - '63)							
Mantadoc	1967	BC	D	17,650	607' 09"	62' 00"	36' 00"
Paterson	1985	BC	D	32,600	736' 06"	75' 10"	42' 00"
Quedoc	1965	BC	D	28,050	730' 00"	75' 00"	39' 02"
(Beavercliffe Hall '65 - '88)							
(Last operated December 20, 1991 — Laid up in Thunder Bay, ON)							
Vandoc	1964	BC	D	16,000	605' 00"	62' 00"	33' 10"
(Sir Denys Lowson '64 - '79)							
(Last operated December 21, 1991 — Laid up in Thunder Bay, ON)							
Windoc	1959	BC	D	29,100	730' 00"	75' 09"	40' 02"
(Rhine Ore '59 - '76, Steelcliffe Hall '76 - '88)							

Roger Blough enters the Duluth Ship Canal.

Kim Nolan

Fleet No. and Name Vessel Name	Year Built	Type of Ship	Type of Engine	Cargo Cap. or Gross*	Length	Beam	Depth or Draft*
P-3 — PETERSON'S BUILDERS, INC., STURGEON BAY, WI							
Escort I	1955	TB	D		50' 00"	15' 00"	7' 03"
Escort II	1969	TB	D		50' 00"	13' 00"	7' 00"
PBI No. 1	1957	DB	B	200*	96' 00"	36' 00"	7' 00"
P-4 — PITTS INTERNATIONAL, INC., DON MILLS, ON							
Flo Cooper	1962	TB	D	97*	80' 00"	21' 00"	10' 09"
P-5 — PLACE RESOURCES CORP., NANTICOKE, ON							
Toni D.	1959	TB	D	15*	50' 00"	16' 00"	5' 00"
P-6 — J. W. PURVIS MARINE LTD., SAULT STE. MARIE, ON							
Yankcanuck	1963	CS	D	4,760	324' 03"	49' 00"	26' 00"
Adanac	1913	TB	D	108*	80' 03"	19' 00"	10' 06"
Anglian Lady	1972	TB	D	398*	136' 06"	30' 00"	14' 01"
Avenger IV	1962	TB	D	293*	120' 00"	30' 05"	17' 05"
Wilfred M. Cohen	1946	TB	D	284*	104' 00"	28' 00"	14' 06"
Goki	1940	TB	D	24*	57' 00"	12' 08"	7' 00"
Martin E. Johnson	1959	TB	D	26*	46' 00"	16' 00"	5' 09"
Miseford	1915	TB	D	116*	85' 00"	20' 00"	10' 06"
W. I. Scott Purvis	1938	TB	D	191*	100' 06"	25' 06"	9' 00"
W. J. Ivan Purvis	1938	TB	D	191*	100' 06"	25' 06"	9' 00"
Rocket	1901	TB	D	39*	70' 00"	15' 00"	8' 00"
Chief Wawatam	1911	DB	B	4,500	347' 00"	62' 03"	15' 00"
G.L.B. No. 2	1953	DB	B	3,215	290' 00"	50' 00"	12' 00"
Charles W. Johnson	1916	DB	B	1,685	245' 00"	43' 00"	14' 00"
Malden	1946	DB	B	1,075	150' 00"	41' 09"	10' 03"
McAllister 132	1954	DB	B	7,000	343' 00"	63' 00"	19' 00"
McKeller	1935	DB	B	200	90' 00"	33' 00"	8' 00"
P.M.L. Alton	1951	DB	B	150	93' 00"	30' 00"	8' 00"
P.M.L. Salvager	1945	DB	B	5,200	341' 00"	54' 00"	27' 00"
Q-1 — QMT NAVIGATION, INC., MONTREAL, PQ							
W. M. Vacy Ash	1969	TK	D	71,500	399' 09"	60' 09"	29' 09"
(Lakeshell '69 - '87)							
IMPERIAL OIL LTD. — MANAGED							
Le Brave	1977	TK	D	78,000	431' 05"	65' 07"	35' 05"
(Texaco Brave '77 - '86)							
Q-2 — QUEBEC TUGS LTD., QUEBEC, PQ							
Capt. Ioannis S.	1973	TB	D	722*	136' 08"	35' 08"	22' 00"
Donald P.	1970	TB	D	320*	110' 00"	28' 06"	17' 00"
Leonard W.	1973	TB	D	448*	123' 02"	33' 00"	18' 09"
Laval	1969	TB	D	438*	104' 08"	35' 05"	18' 00"
R-1 — REMORQUEURS ET BARGES MONTREAL LTEE., VALLEYFIELD, PQ							
Cavalier	1944	TB	D	18*	40' 00"	10' 05"	4' 08"
Flo-Mac	1960	TB	D	18*	40' 00"	13' 00"	6' 00"
Glenside	1944	TB	D	91*	81' 00"	21' 00"	9' 00"
Greta V	1951	TB	D	14*	44' 00"	12' 00"	5' 00"
Argue Martin	1895	TB	D	71*	69' 00"	19' 06"	9' 00"

Fleet No. and Name Vessel Name	Year Built	Type of Ship	Type of Engine	Cargo Cap. or Gross*	Length	Beam	Depth or Draft*
Plainsville	1944	TB	D	18*	40' 00"	10' 05"	4' 08"
Robert B. No. 1	1956	TB	D	170*	91' 00"	27' 00"	12' 00"

R-2 — ROEN SALVAGE CO., STURGEON BAY, WI

Chas Asher	1956	TB	D	10*	50' 00"	18' 00"	8' 00"
John R. Asher	1943	TB	D	93*	70' 00"	20' 00"	8' 06"
Stephen M. Asher	1954	TB	D	60*	65' 00"	19' 01"	5' 04"
Louie S.	1914	TB	D	43*	37' 00"	12' 00"	5' 00"
Spuds	1946	TB	D	19*	42' 00"	12' 06"	6' 00"
Timmy A.	1953	TB	D	12*	33' 06"	10' 08"	5' 02"

Note: Various deck and crane barges are available.

R-3 — RYBA MARINE CONSTRUCTION CO., CHEBOYGAN, MI

Kathy Lynn	1944	TB	D	140*	85' 00"	24' 00"	9' 06"
Venture	1922	TB	D	67*	65' 00"	14' 01"	10' 00"
Harbor Master	1979	DB	B	100*	70' 00"	27' 00"	4' 00"
Jarco 1402	1981	CB	B	600	140' 01"	39' 01"	8' 06"
No. 4	1956	DB	B	277*	120' 00"	42' 00"	9' 00"
Tonawanda	1935	DB	B	375*	120' 00"	45' 00"	8' 00"

S-1 — ST. LAWRENCE SEAWAY DEVELOPMENT CORP., MASSENA, NY

Eighth Sea	1958	TB	D	17*	40' 00"	12' 06"	4' 00"
Fourth Coast	1957	TB	D	17*	40' 00"	12' 06"	4' 00"
Robinson Bay	1958	TB	D	213*	103' 00"	27' 00"	12' 06"

S-2 — ST. LAWRENCE TUG BOATS, INC., MONTREAL, PQ

Jerry G.	1960	TB	D	202*	91' 06"	27' 03"	12' 06"

S-3 — ST. MARY'S CEMENT CO., TORONTO, ON

Sea Eagle II	1979	TB	D	560*	132' 00"	35' 00"	19' 00"
St. Mary's Cement II	1978	CC	B	18,500	496' 06"	76' 00"	35' 00"
St. Mary's Cement III	1980	CC	B	4,800	335' 00"	76' 08"	17' 09"

(Bigorange XVI '80 - '85, Says '85 - '85, Al-Sayb-7 '85 - '86, Clarkson Carrier '86 - '94)

S-4 — ST. MARY'S HOLDINGS, INC., DETROIT, MI

St. Mary's Cement	1986	CC	B	9,400	360' 00"	60' 00"	23' 03"

S-5 — SEARS OIL CO., INC., ROME, NY

Midstate I	1942	TB	D	106*	86' 00"	24' 00"	12' 00"
Midstate II	1945	TB	D	137*	89' 00"	24' 00"	12' 06"

S-6 — SELVICK MARINE TOWING CORP., STURGEON BAY, WI

Baldy B.	1932	TB	D	36*	62' 00"	16' 01"	7' 00"
Mary Page Hannah	1949	TB	D	461*	143' 00"	33' 01"	14' 06"
Bonnie G. Selvick	1928	TB	D	95*	86' 00"	21' 06"	12' 00"
Carl William Selvick	1947	TB	D	473*	143' 00"	34' 00"	17' 00"
Carla Anne Selvick	1970	TB	D	193*	96' 00"	23' 00"	12' 00"
John M. Selvick	1898	TB	D	256*	118' 00"	24' 03"	16' 00"
Sharon M. Selvick	1945	TB	D	28*	45' 06"	13' 00"	7' 01"
William C. Selvick	1944	TB	D	142*	86' 03"	23' 00"	11' 00"
Moby Dick	1952	DB	B	835	121' 00"	33' 02"	10' 06"

Fleet No. and Name Vessel Name	Year Built	Type of Ship	Type of Engine	Cargo Cap. or Gross*	Length	Beam	Depth or Draft*

S-7 — SHELL CANADA PRODUCTS LTD., MONTREAL, PQ
Horizon Montreal	1958	TK	D	32,900	315' 00"	45' 07"	24' 07"
(Tyee Shell '58 - '69, Artic Trader '69 - '83, Rivershell '83 - '95)							

S-8 — SOCANAV, INC., MONTREAL, PQ
Hubert Gaucher	1982	TK	D	91,252	444' 06"	64' 00"	32' 09"
(L'erable No.1 '82 - '82)							
L' Orme No. 1	1974	TK	D	68,000	432' 09"	60' 00"	28' 00"
(Leon Simard '74 - '82)							
Le Chene No. 1	1961	TK	D	64,580	430' 07"	52' 00"	28' 00"
(J. Edouard Simard '61 - '67, Edouard Simard '67 - '82)							
Le Saule No. 1	1970	TK	D	63,000	412' 06"	52' 00"	28' 00"
(Ludger Simard '70 - '82)							

OLYMPUS NAVIGATION, INC.
Icepurha	1968	TK	D		619' 00"	72' 04"	47' 11"

IMPERIAL OIL LTD. — MANAGED
A. G. Farquharson	1969	TK	D	53,000	400' 06"	54' 02"	26' 05"
(Texaco Chief '69 - '86)							

S-9 — SOREL TUG BOATS, INC., SOREL, PQ
Omni-Richlieu	1969	TB	D	134*	79' 06"	24' 06"	11' 04"
Omni-St. Laurent	1957	TB	D	161*	90' 03"	24' 09"	12' 08"

T-1 — THUNDER BAY MARINE SERVICE LTD., THUNDER BAY, ON
Coastal Cruiser	1939	TB	D	29*	65' 00"	18' 00"	12' 00"
Glenada	1944	TB	D	107*	80' 06"	25' 00"	10' 01"
Robert W.	1949	TB	D	48*	60' 00"	16' 00"	8' 06"
Rosalee D.	1943	TB	D	22*	55' 00"	16' 00"	10' 00"
Agoming	1926	DB	B	200	100' 00"	34' 00"	8' 06"

T-2 — THUNDER BAY TUG SERVICES LTD., THUNDER BAY, ON
Point Valour	1958	TB	D	247*	97' 06"	26' 01"	13' 10"

T-3 — TORONTO CITY FIRE DEPT., TORONTO, ON
William Lyon Mackenzie		FB	D	100*	81' 00"	20' 00"	10' 00"

T-4 — TORONTO HARBOUR COMMISSIONERS, TORONTO, ON
J. G. Langton	1934	TB	D	15*	45' 00"	12' 00"	5' 00"
William Rest	1961	TB	D	62*	65' 00"	18' 06"	10' 06"
Fred Scandrett	1963	TB	D	52*	62' 00"	17' 00"	8' 00"

T-5 — TRANSPORT DESGAGNES, INC., QUEBEC, PQ
CROISIERES NORDIK
Nordik Passeur	1962	CF	D	60 pass	283' 10"	60' 05"	20' 00"
(Confederation '62 - '93, Hull - 28 '93 - '94)							

GROUP DESGAGNES
Amelia Desgagnes	1976	CS	D	7,000	355' 00"	49' 00"	30' 06"
(Soodoc '76 - '90)							
Catherine Desgagnes	1962	BC	D	8,350	410' 03"	56' 04"	31' 00"
(Gosforth '62 - '72, Thorold '72 - '85)							
Cecelia Desgagnes	1971	BC	D	7,875	374' 10"	54' 10"	34' 06"
(Carl Gorthon '71 - '81, Federal Pioneer '81 - '85)							

John J. Boland arrives at the CSX #4 coal dock, Toledo, 25 June, 1995.

Angela S. Clayton

Fleet No. and Name Vessel Name	Year Built	Type of Ship	Type of Engine	Cargo Cap. or Gross*	Length	Beam	Depth or Draft*
J. A. Z. Desgagnes	1960	BC	D	1,250	208' 10"	36' 00"	14' 00"
(Vison Consol '60 - '74)							
Jacques Desgagnes	1960	BC	D	1,250	208' 10"	36' 00"	14' 00"
(Loutre Consol '60 - '77)							
Mathilda Desgagnes	1959	BC	D	6,920	360' 00"	51' 00"	30' 02"
(Eskimo '59 - '80)							
Melissa Desgagnes	1975	CS	D	7,000	355' 00"	49' 00"	30' 06"
(Ontadoc '75 - '90)							
Thalassa Desgagnes	1976	TK	D	58,000	441' 05"	56' 07"	32' 10"
(Orinoco '76 - '79, Joasla '79 - '82, Rio Orinoco '82 - '93)							

RELAIS NORDIK

Nordik Express	1974		D				
(Theriot Offshore IV '74 - '77, Scotoil '77 - '79, Tartan Sea '79 - '87)							

T-6 — TROIS RIVIERES REMORQUEURS LTEE., TROIS RIVIERES, PQ

Andre H.	1963	TB	D	317*	126' 00"	28' 06"	15' 06"
Duga	1977	TB	D	402*	111' 00"	33' 00"	16' 01"
R. F. Grant	1969	TB	D	78*	71' 00"	17' 00"	8' 00"
Robert H.	1944	TB	D	400*	111' 00"	27' 00"	13' 00"

U-1 — UNDERWATER GAS DEVELOPERS, PORT COLBORNE, ON

C. West Pete	1956	TB	D	29*	63' 00"	17' 03"	5' 06"

U-2 — U.S. ARMY CORPS OF ENGINEERS, DETROIT, MI

Bayfield	1953	TB	D		45' 00"	13' 00"	6' 00"
Buffalo	1953	TB	D		45' 00"	13' 00"	7' 00"
Duluth	1954	TB	D		70' 00"	20' 00"	8' 06"
Fairchild	1953	TB	D		45' 00"	13' 00"	5' 01"
Forney	1944	TB	D		86' 00"	23' 00"	10' 00"
Owen M. Frederick	1942	TB	D		65' 00"	17' 00"	7' 00"
Hammond Bay	1953	TB	D		45' 00"	13' 00"	6' 00"
Houghton	1944	TB	D		45' 00"	13' 00"	6' 00"
Kenosha	1954	TB	D		70' 00"	20' 00"	8' 06"
Lake Superior	1943	TB	D		113' 00"	26' 00"	14' 00"
Ludington	1943	TB	D		114' 00"	26' 00"	12' 02"
Natchitoches	1970	TB	D	356*	109' 00"	30' 06"	16' 06"
Racine	1931	TB	D		66' 00"	18' 00"	6' 08"
Rouge	1955	TB	D		71' 00"	20' 00"	8' 04"
Shelter Bay	1953	TB	D		45' 00"	13' 00"	5' 00"
Stanley	1944	TB	D		86' 00"	23' 00"	10' 00"
Tawas Bay	1953	TB	D		45' 00"	13' 00"	5' 00"
Washington	1952	TB	D		107' 00"	26' 06"	15' 00"
Whitefish Bay	1953	TB	D		45' 00"	13' 00"	5' 00"
James M. Bray	1986	SV	D		128' 00"	31' 00"	5' 07"
Paj	1986	SV	D		120' 00"	33' 00"	2' 06"

Barges: Coleman, Harvey, Huron, Manitowoc, Markus, McCauley, Michigan, Nicolet, Simonsen, H. J. Schwartz, Tonawanda, Paul Bunyan

U-3 — U.S. COAST GUARD - 9TH COAST GUARD DIST., CLEVELAND, OH

Biscayne Bay	1979	IB	D	662*	140' 00"	37' 06"	12' 00"*
Bristol Bay	1979	IB	D	662*	140' 00"	37' 06"	12' 00"*
Katmai Bay	1978	IB	D	662*	140' 00"	37' 06"	12' 00"*

Fleet No. and Name Vessel Name	Year Built	Type of Ship	Type of Engine	Cargo Cap. or Gross*	Length	Beam	Depth or Draft*
Mackinaw	1944	IB	D	5,252*	290' 00"	74' 00"	19' 00"*
Mobile Bay	1979	IB	D	662*	140' 00"	37' 06"	12' 00"*
Neah Bay	1980	IB	D	662*	140' 00"	37' 06"	12' 00"*
Acacia	1944	BT	D	1,025*	180' 00"	37' 00"	13' 00"*
Bramble	1944	BT	D	1,025*	180' 00"	37' 00"	13' 00"*
Sundew	1944	BT	D	1,025*	180' 00"	37' 00"	13' 00"*
Buckthorn	1963	BT	D	200*	100' 00"	24' 00"	4' 00"*

U-4 — U.S. DEPT. OF THE INTERIOR, U.S. FISH & WILDLIFE SERVICE, ANN ARBOR, MI

Cisco	1951	RV	D		60' 06"	16' 08"	7' 08"
Grayling	1977	RV	D		75' 00"	22' 00"	9' 10"
Kaho	1961	RV	D		64' 10"	17' 10"	9' 00"
Musky II	1960	RV	D	25*	45' 00"	14' 04"	5' 00"
Siscowet	1946	RV	D	54*	57' 00"	14' 06"	7' 00"

U-5 — U.S. ENVIRONMENTAL PROTECTION AGENCY, WASHINGTON D.C.

Lake Guardian	1989	RV	D	282*	180' 00"	40' 00"	11' 00"
(Marsea Fourteen '81 - '90)							
Roger R. Simons	1939	RV	D	375*	122' 00"	28' 00"	8' 00"
(USCGC Maple (WLI-234) '39 - '74)							

U-6 — U. S. NAVAL SEA CADET CORPS, PONTIAC, MI — 810-666-9359

Pride of Michigan	1977	TV	D	70*	80' 06"	7' 08"	5' 03"

U-7 — UPPER LAKES SHIPPING LTD., TORONTO, ON
HAMILTON MARINE DIVISION

James E. McGrath	1963	TB	D	90*	77' 00"	20' 00"	10' 09"

JACKES SHIPPING, INC.

Canadian Trader	1969	BC	D	28,300	730' 00"	75' 00"	39' 08"
(Ottercliffe Hall '69 - '83, Royalton '83 - '85, Ottercliffe Hall '85 - '88, Peter Misener '88 - '94)							
Canadian Venture	1965	BC	D	28,050	730' 00"	75' 00"	39' 02"
(Lawrencecliffe Hall '65 - '88, David K. Gardiner '88 - '94)							
Gordon C. Leitch	1968	BC	D	29,700	730' 00"	75' 00"	42' 00"
(Ralph Misener '68 - '94)							

PROVMAR FUELS, INC.

Hamilton Energy	1965	TK	D	8,622 bbls	201' 05"	34' 01"	14' 09"
(Partington '65 - '79, Shell Scientist '79 - '81, Metro Sun '81 - '85)							
Provmar Terminal	1959	TK	B	60,000 bbls	403' 05"	55' 06"	28' 05"
(Varangnes '59 - '70, Tommy Wiborg '70 - '74, Ungava Transport '74 - '85)							
(Last operated in 1984 — Currently in use as a fuel storage barge in Hamilton, ON)							
Provmar Terminal II	1948	TK	B	56,010 bbls	408' 08"	53' 00"	26' 00"
(Imperial Sarnia '48 - '86)							
(Last operated in 1986 — Currently in use as a fuel storage barge in Hamilton, ON)							

ULS CORPORATION

Canadian Century	1967	SU	D	31,600	730' 00"	75' 00"	45' 00"
Canadian Enterprise	1979	SU	D	35,100	730' 00"	75' 08"	46' 06"
Canadian Explorer	1944	BC	D	26,000	730' 00"	75' 00"	39' 03"
(Verendrye '44 - '47, Edenfield '47 - '61, Northern Venture '61 - '83)							
Canadian Leader	1967	BC	T	28,300	730' 00"	75' 00"	39' 08"
(Feux - Follets '67 - '72)							
Canadian Mariner	1963	BC	T	27,700	730' 00"	75' 00"	39' 03"
(Newbrunswicker '63 - '68, Grande Hermine '68 - '72)							

Fleet No. and Name Vessel Name	Year Built	Type of Ship	Type of Engine	Cargo Cap. or Gross*	Length	Beam	Depth or Draft*
Canadian Miner	1966	BC	D	28,050	730' 00"	75' 00"	39' 01"
(Maplecliffe Hall '66 - '88, Lemoyne '88 - '94)							
Canadian Navigator	1967	BC	D	31,600	729' 10"	75' 10"	40' 06"
(Demeterton '67 - '75, St. Lawrence Navigator '75 - '80)							
Canadian Olympic	1976	SU	D	35,100	730' 00"	75' 00"	46' 06"
Canadian Progress	1968	SU	D	32,700	730' 00"	75' 00"	46' 06"
Canadian Prospector	1964	BC	D	30,500	730' 00"	75' 10"	40' 06"
(Carlton '64 - '75, St. Lawrence Prospector '75 - '79)							
Canadian Provider	1963	BC	T	27,450	730' 00"	75' 00"	39' 02"
(Murray Bay '63 - '94)							
Canadian Ranger	1943	GU	D	25,900	730' 00"	75' 00"	39' 03"
(Grande Ronde '43 - '48, Kate N. L. '48 - '61, Hilda Marjanne '61 - '84)							
Canadian Transport	1979	SU	D	35,100	730' 00"	75' 08"	46' 06"
Canadian Voyager	1963	BC	T	27,050	730' 00"	75' 00"	39' 02"
(Black Bay '63 - '94)							
Hamilton Transfer	1943	SU	B	15,650	620' 06"	60' 00"	35' 00"
(J. H. Hillman Jr. '43 - '74, Crispin Oglebay '74 - '95)							
(Last operated May 29, 1991 — Currently in use as a transfer barge in Hamilton, ON)							
Montrealais	1962	BC	T	27,800	730' 00"	75' 00"	39' 00"
(Montrealer '62 - '62)							
James Norris	1952	SU	U	18,600	663' 06"	67' 00"	35' 00"
Quebecois	1963	BC	T	27,800	730' 00"	75' 00"	39' 00"
Seaway Queen	1959	BC	T	24,300	713' 03"	72' 00"	37' 00"
ULS MARBULK, INC.							
Ambassador	1983	SU	D	37,800	730' 00"	75' 10"	50' 00"
(Canadian Ambassador '83 - '85)							
Citadel Hill	1967	SU	D	50,000	700' 00"	96' 02"	55' 00"
(Thorsdrake '67 - '75, Cape Breton Highlander '75 - '80, Canadian Highlander '80 - '83)							
Nelvana	1983	SU	D	75,000	797' 00"	106' 00"	65' 00"
Pioneer	1981	SU	D	37,900	730' 00"	75' 10"	50' 00"
(Canadian Pioneer '81 - '86)							
Richmond Hill	1981	BC	D	38,000	635' 10"	90' 06"	52' 00"
(Frotacanada '81 - '87, Porthos '87 - '89, Nai Ookkam '89 - '93)							
Thornhill	1981	BC	D	38,000	635' 10"	90' 06"	52' 00"
(Frotabrasil '81 - '87, Athos '87 - '89, Chennai Perumai '89 - '93)							

U-8 — UPPER LAKES TOWING, INC., ESCANABA, MI

William H. Donner	1914	CS	B	9,400	524' 00"	54' 00"	30' 00"
(Last operated in 1969 — Currently laid up in Menominee, MI)							
Olive M. Moore	1928	TB	D	297*	125' 00"	27' 01"	13' 09"
Joseph H. Thompson	1944	SU	B	21,200	706' 06"	71' 06"	38' 06"
(Marine Robin '44 - '52)							
Joseph H. Thompson Jr.	1990	TB	D	841*	146' 06"	38' 00"	35' 00"

LAKES SHIPPING SERVICE CO. — MANAGED

McKee Sons	1945	SU	B	19,900	579' 02"	71' 06"	38' 06"
(Marine Angel '45 - '53)							

U-9 — USS GREAT LAKES FLEET, INC., DULUTH, MN

Arthur M. Anderson	1952	SU	T	25,300	767' 00"	70' 00"	36' 00"
Roger Blough	1972	SU	D	43,900	858' 00"	105' 00"	41' 06"

John Vournakis

Stern view of the tug-barge combination Presque Isle shows how the two hulls fit securely together.

Fleet No. and Name / Vessel Name	Year Built	Type of Ship	Type of Engine	Cargo Cap. or Gross*	Length	Beam	Depth or Draft*
Calcite II	1929	SU	D	12,650	604' 09"	60' 00"	32' 00"
(William G. Clyde '29 - '61)							
Cason J. Callaway	1952	SU	T	25,300	767' 00"	70' 00"	36' 00"
Philip R. Clarke	1952	SU	T	25,300	767' 00"	70' 00"	36' 00"
Edwin H. Gott	1979	SU	D	74,100	1,004' 00"	105' 00"	56' 00"
John G. Munson	1952	SU	T	25,550	768' 03"	72' 00"	36' 00"
Ojibway	1945	SB	D	65*	53' 00"	28' 00"	7' 00"
George A. Sloan	1943	SU	D	15,800	620' 06"	60' 00"	35' 00"
(Hill Annex '43 - '43)							
Edgar B. Speer	1980	SU	D	73,700	1,004' 00"	105' 00"	56' 00"
Myron C. Taylor	1929	SU	D	12,450	603' 09"	60' 00"	32' 00"
LITTON GREAT LAKES CORP. — MANAGED							
Presque Isle	1973	TB	D	1,578*	153' 03"	54' 00"	31' 03"
Presque Isle	1973	SU	B	57,500	974' 06"	104' 07"	46' 06"
(Overall Dimensions Together)				1,000' 00"	104' 07"	46' 06"	

W-1 — WATERMAN'S SERVICES LTD., TORONTO, ON

Colinette	1943	TB	D	64*	65' 00"	16' 00"	7' 00"
Duchess V	1955	TB	D	18*	55' 00"	16' 00"	6' 08"

W-2 — J. W. WESTCOTT CO., DETROIT, MI

J. W. Westcott II	1949	MB	D	11*	46' 01"	13' 09"	4' 09"

W-3 — WISCONSIN & MICHIGAN STEAMSHIP CO., DETROIT, MI

Highway 16	1942	AC	D	190 cars	328' 00"	50' 00"	25' 00"
(USS LST 393 '42 - '48)				*(Currently laid up in Muskegon, MI)*			

W-4 — UNIVERSITY OF WISCONSIN

L. Lloyd Smith Jr.	1950	RV	D	38*	58' 00"	16' 06"	6' 00"

Angela S. Clayton

Cement carrier Alpena displays her graceful lines.

Jim Hoffman

Great Lakes Towing Co. tug South Carolina helps the Canadian Provider at Toledo.

Fleet No. and Name / Vessel Name	Year Built	Type of Ship	Type of Engine	Cargo Cap. or Gross*	Length	Beam	Depth or Draft*
PA-1 — ADVENTURES AFLOAT, TORONTO, ON							
Torontonian	ES	1962	D	175 pass	55' 00"	17' 00"	4' 00"
PA-2 - AMERICAN CANADIAN CARIBBEAN LINE, INC., WARREN, RI							
Caribbean Prince	PA	1983	D	80 pass	160' 00"	38' 00"	6' 00"
Mayan Prince	PA	1992	D	96 pass	175' 00"	38' 00"	9' 08"
Niagara Prince	PA	1994	D	84 pass	166' 00"	38' 00"	6' 00"
PA-3 — APOSTLE ISLAND CRUISE SERVICE, BAYFIELD, WI							
Manitou	ES		D	150 pass			
Sea Queen II	ES	1971	D	49 pass	42' 00"	14' 00"	2' 07"
PA-4 — ARNOLD TRANSIT CO., MACKINAC ISLAND, MI							
Algomah	PF	1961	D	600 pass	95' 00"	31' 00"	8' 00"
Chippewa	PF	1962	D	600 pass	91' 00"	29' 08"	8' 00"
Corsair	CF	1955	D	190 pass	91' 00"	33' 00"	6' 05"
Huron	PF	1957	D	400 pass	91' 06"	25' 00"	10' 01"
Island Express	PF	1986	D	380 pass	82' 05"	28' 05"	6' 08"
Mackinac Express	PF	1986	D	350 pass	82' 05"	28' 05"	6' 08"
Ottawa	PF	1959	D	600 pass	95' 00"	31' 00"	8' 00"
Straits Express	PF	1995	D	400 pass	98' 00"	30' 00"	6' 08"
Straits of Mackinac II	PF	1969	D	446 pass	89' 11"	27' 00"	8' 08"
PB-1 — BEAVER ISLAND BOAT COMPANY, CHARLEVOIX, MI							
Beaver Islander	PF	1963	D	200 pass	96' 03"	9' 09"	7' 03"
South Shore	PF	1945	D	120 pass	64' 09"	24' 00"	9' 06"
Emerald Isle	PF	1996	D	300 pass			
PB-2 — BLUE WATER EXCURSIONS, INC., PORT HURON, MI							
Huron Lady	ES	1961	D	109 pass	65' 00"	17' 00"	5' 00"
PB-3— BLUE WATER FERRY LTD., SOMBRA, ON							
Daldean	CF	1951	D	125 pass	75' 00"	35' 00"	7' 00"
Ontamich	CF	1939	D	40 pass	65' 00"	29' 00"	8' 06"
PC-1 — CANAMAC CRUISES, TORONTO, ON							
Aurora Borealis	ES	1981	D	200 pass	106' 00"		6' 00"
PC-2 — JACQUES CARTIER, INC., TROIS RIVIERES, PQ							
Jacques Cartier	ES	1924	D	380 pass	135' 00"	35' 00"	10' 00"
PC-3 — CEDAR POINT TRANSPORTATION, SANDUSKY, OH							
Cedar Point	PF	1952	D	110 pass	65' 00"	16' 06"	4' 00"
Cedar Point II	PF	1953	D	115 pass	65' 00"	17' 00"	4' 00"
Cedar Point III	PF	1952	D	110 pass	65' 00"	16' 06"	4' 00"
PC-4 — CHAMPION AUTO FERRY, ALGONAC, MI							
Champion	CF	1941	D	80 pass	72' 09"	29' 00"	8' 06"
North Channel	CF	1967	D	102 pass	75' 00"	30' 06"	8' 00"
St. Clair Flats	CF	1946	D	80 pass	73' 00"	29' 00"	8' 03"
South Channel	CF	1973	D	100 pass	79' 00"	30' 03"	8' 06"

Passenger liner Keewatin, nearing the end of her days in the early 1960s. She is now a museum at Douglas, MI.

Tom Manse

Fleet No. and Name Vessel Name	Year Built	Type of Ship	Type of Engine	Cargo Cap. or Gross*	Length	Beam	Depth or Draft*
PC-5 — CHARLEVOIX COUNTY ROAD COMM., CHARLEVOIX, MI							
Charlevoix	CF	1926	D	35 pass	50' 00"	32' 00"	3' 09"
PC-6 — G.R. CLOUTIER, LONGUEUIL, PQ							
Miss Montreal	ES	1973	D	50 pass	70' 00"	20' 00"	6' 00"
PC-7 — CONTESSA CRUISE LINES, EDEN PRAIRIE, MN							
Arthur K. Atkinson	PA	1917	D	112 pass	384' 00"	56' 00"	20' 06"
(Ann Arbor No. 6 '17 - '59)							
(Last operated in 1984 — Currently laid up in Ludington, MI)							
Viking	PA	1925	D	350 pass	360' 00"	56' 03"	21' 06"
(Ann Arbor No. 7 '25 - '64)							
(Last operated April 11, 1982 — Currently laid up in Manitowoc, WI)							
PC-8 — CROISIERES MARJOLAINE, INC., CHICOUTIMI, PQ							
Marjolaine II	ES	1904	D	175 pass	92' 00"	27' 00"	9' 00"
PC-9 - CROSISIERE DES ISLES DE SOREL, INC., STE. ANNE DE SOREL, PQ							
Le Survenant III	ES	1948	D	185 pass	60' 00"	13' 00"	5' 00"
PD-1 — DIAMOND JACK'S RIVER TOURS, DETROIT, MI							
Diamond Belle	ES	1958	D	400 pass	93' 06"	25' 10"	10' 00"
Diamond Jack	ES	1955	D	250 pass	63' 00"	25' 00"	7' 03"
Diamond Queen	ES	1956	D	400 pass	93' 00"	25' 00"	10' 00"
PD-2 — DENNIS DOUGHERTY, SAULT STE. MARIE, MI							
Gerald D. Neville	TB	1924	D	29*	50' 00"	13' 00"	4' 06"
(Tobermory '24 - '41, Champion '41 - '81)							
PD-3 — DUC D' ORLEANS CRUISE BOAT, SARNIA, ON							
Duc D' Orleans	ES	1944	D	200 pass	112' 00"	18' 00"	9' 00"
PE-1 — EASTERN UPPER PENINSULA TRANSIT AUTH., KINCHELOE, MI							
Drummond Islander	CF	1947	D	142 pass	84' 00"	30' 00"	8' 03"
Drummond Islander III	CF	1989	D	152 pass	108' 00"	37' 00"	12' 03"
Neebish Islander	CF	1950	D	26 pass	55' 00"	20' 07"	6' 00"
Neebish Islander II	CF	1946	D	114 pass	89' 00"	29' 06"	6' 09"
Sugar Islander II	CF	1995	D	140 pass	114' 00"	40' 00"	10' 00"
Thunder Bay	TB	1953	D	15*	45' 00"	13' 00"	7' 00"
PE-2 — EDELWEISS CRUISE DINING, MILWAUKEE, WI							
Edelweiss I	ES	1988	D	100 pass	64' 08"	18' 00"	6' 00"
Edelweiss II	ES	1989	D	149 pass	73' 08"	20' 00"	7' 00"
PE-3 — EMPIRE CRUISE LINES, U. S. A.							
Marine Star	PA	1945	T	2,500 pass	520' 00"	71' 06"	26' 00"
(Marine Star '45 - '55, Aquarama '55 - '94)							
(Last operated in 1963 — Currently laid up in Buffalo, NY)							
PG-1 — GANANOQUE BOAT LINE, GANANOQUE, ON							
Thousand Islander	ES	1972	D	580 pass	100' 00"	22' 00"	5' 00"
Thousand Islander II	ES	1973	D	370 pass	110' 00"	22' 00"	5' 00"

Fleet No. and Name Vessel Name	Year Built	Type of Ship	Type of Engine	Cargo Cap. or Gross*	Length	Beam	Depth or Draft*
Thousand Islander III	ES	1975	D	500 pass	119' 00"	22' 00"	6' 00"
Thousand Islander IV	ES	1976	D	500 pass	118' 00"	28' 00"	6' 00"

PG-2 — GOODTIME ISLAND CRUISES, INC., SANDUSKY, OH
Goodtime I	ES	1964	D	365 pass	111' 00"	24' 00"	9' 05"

PG-3 — GOODTIME TRANSIT BOATS, INC., CLEVELAND, OH
Goodtime III	ES	1990	D	1,000 pass	161' 00"	40' 00"	11' 00"

PG-4 — GRAND PORTAGE - ISLE ROYALE TRANS. LINES, DULUTH, MN
A. E. Clifford	ES	1946	D	50 pass	45' 00"	15' 00"	7' 00"
Hiawatha	ES	1938	D	50 pass	58' 00"	15' 00"	8' 00"
Provider	ES	1959	D	50 pass	46' 00"	13' 05"	5' 05"
Voyageur II	ES	1970	D	49 pass	63' 00"	18' 00"	5' 00"
Wenonah	ES	1960	D	150 pass	64' 09"	20' 00"	7' 00"

PH-1 — HARBOR LIGHT CRUISE LINES, TOLEDO, OH
Sandpiper	ES	1984	D	101 pass	65' 00"	16' 00"	4' 00"

PH-2 — HORNE'S FERRY, WOLFE ISLAND, ON
William Darrell	CF	1952	D	45 pass	66' 00"	28' 00"	6' 00"

PH-3 — HOWE ISLAND TOWNSHIP, GANANOQUE, ON
The Howe Islander	CF	1946	D	25 pass	53' 00"	12' 00"	3' 00"

PI-1 — INLAND SEAS EDUCATION ASSOC., SUTTONS BAY, MI
Inland Seas	RV	1994	SAIL	41*	61' 06"	17' 00"	7' 00"

PI-2 — IROQUOIS BOAT LINE CO., MILWAUKEE, WI
Iroquois	ES	1946	D	149 pass	61' 09"	21' 00"	6' 04"

PI-3 — IVY LEA 1000 ISLANDS BOAT TOURS, IVY LEA, ON
Miss Ivy Lea II	ES		D	100 pass	66' 00"	15' 00"	5' 00"
Miss Ivy Lea III	ES		D	76 pass	48' 00"	12' 00"	5' 00"

PK-1 — KELLEY'S ISLAND FERRY BOAT LINES, MARBLEHEAD, OH
Erie Isle	CF	1951	D	180 pass	72' 00"	24' 00"	8' 03"
Shirley Irene	CF	1991	D	150 pass	160' 00"	46' 00"	9' 00"

PK-2 — D. E. KILPELA ISLE ROYALE FERRY SERVICE, INC., COPPER HARBOR, MI
Isle Royale Queen II	PF	1959	D	54 pass	85' 00"	18' 04"	9' 05"

PL-1 - LAKE MICHIGAN CARFERRY SERV., INC., LUDINGTON, MI
Badger (43)	CF	1953	S	520 pass	410' 06"	59' 06"	24' 00"
City of Midland 41	CF	1941	S	609 pass	406' 00"	58' 00"	23' 06"

(Last operated November 18, 1988 — Currently laid up in Ludington, MI)

Spartan (42)	CF	1952	S	520 pass	410' 06"	59' 06"	24' 00"

(Last operated January 20, 1979 — Currently laid up in Ludington, MI)

PL-2 — LEE MARINE LTD., PORT LAMBTON, ON
Hammond Bay	ES	1992	D	43*	54' 00"	16' 00"	3' 06"
Nancy A. Lee	TB	1939	D	9*	40' 00"	12' 00"	3' 00"

Fleet No. and Name / Vessel Name	Year Built	Type of Ship	Type of Engine	Cargo Cap. or Gross*	Length	Beam	Depth or Draft*
PL-3 — LOCK TOURS CANADA, SAULT STE. MARIE, ON							
Chief Shingwauk	ES	1965	D	200 pass	70' 00"	24' 00"	4' 06"
PM-1 — MADELINE ISLAND FERRY LINE, INC., LAPOINTE, WI							
Island Queen	CF	1966	D	150 pass	75' 00"	34' 09"	10' 00"
Madeline	CF	1984	D	150 pass	90' 00"	35' 00"	8' 00"
Nichevo II	CF	1962	D	150 pass	65' 00"	32' 00"	8'09"
PM-2 — MAID OF THE MIST STEAMBOAT CO. LTD., NIAGARA FALLS, ON							
Maid of the Mist	ES	1987	D	100 pass	65' 00"	16' 00"	7' 00"
Maid of the Mist III	ES	1972	D	150 pass	65' 00"	16' 00"	7' 00"
Maid of the Mist IV	ES	1976	D	200 pass	65' 00"	16' 00"	7' 00"
Maid of the Mist V	ES	1989	D	300 pass	65' 00"	16' 00"	7' 00"
Maid of the Mist VI	ES	1990	D	300 pass	65' 00"	16' 00"	7' 00"
Maid of the Mist VII	ES	1997	D	600 pass	80' 00"	30' 00"	7' 00"
PM-3 — MANITOU ISLAND TRANSIT, LELAND, MI							
Manitou Island	PF	1946	D	67 pass	52' 00"	14' 00"	8' 00"
Mishe-Mokwa	PF	1966	D	110 pass	65' 00"	17' 06"	8' 00"
PM-4 — MARINE ATLANTIC, INC., MONCTON, NB							
Abegweit	CF	1982	D	900 pass	403' 09"	71' 02"	20' 04"
Atlantic Freighter	CF	1978	D	12,162	498' 03"	71' 06"	24' 00"
Sir Robert Bond	CF	1975	D	10,433	446' 06"	71' 06"	16' 08"
Blue Nose	CF	1973	D	1,000 pass	412' 01"	77' 02"	18' 01"
Caribou	CF	1986	D	1,200 pass	590' 07"	84' 04"	21' 05"
John Hamilton Gray	CF	1968	D	516 pass	402' 09"	69' 06"	20' 04"
Holiday Island	CF	1971	D	3,037	323' 00"	68' 06"	16' 05"
Marine Evangeline	CF	1974	D	2,794	363' 04"	57' 09"	40' 06"
Princess of Acadia	CF	1971	D	650 pass	482' 07"	66' 01"	15' 01"
Joseph & Clara Smallwood	CF	1990	D	1,200 pass	590' 07"	84' 04"	21' 05"
Taverner	BC	1962	D	1,135	189' 05"	38' 09"	12' 05"
Vacationland	CF	1971	D	485 pass			
PM-5 — MARIPOSA CRUISE LINE, TORONTO, ON							
Mariposa Belle	ES	1970	D	250 pass	72' 00"	24' 00"	8' 00"
PM-6 — MERCURY CRUISE LINES, CHICAGO, IL							
Chicago's First Lady	ES	1991	D	222 pass	96' 00"	22' 00"	5' 00"
Skyline Princess	ES	1956	D	110 pass	65' 00"	17' 00"	4' 00"
Skyline Queen	ES	1959	D	127 pass	66' 00"	17' 08"	4' 09"
PM-7 — MILLER BOAT LINE, INC., PUT-IN-BAY, OH							
Islander	CF	1983	D	448 pass	90' 03"	38' 00"	8' 03"
Wm. Market	CF	1993	D	500 pass	96' 00"	38' 06"	8' 09"
William M. Miller	CF	1954	D	250 pass	64' 09"	32' 09"	9' 09"
South Bass	CF	1989	D	500 pass	64' 09"	24' 00"	9' 06"
West Shore	CF	1947	D	244 pass	64' 09"	30' 06"	9' 03"
PM-8 — MUSKOKA LAKES NAV. & HOTEL CO., ON							
Segwun	PA	1887	R	168*	128' 00"	22' 00"	8' 00"

Fleet No. and Name Vessel Name	Year Built	Type of Ship	Type of Engine	Cargo Cap. or Gross*	Length	Beam	Depth or Draft*

PN-1 — NEUMAN BOAT LINE, INC., SANDUSKY, OH

Vessel	Type	Year	Eng	Cap	Length	Beam	Depth
Challenger	CF	1947	D	250 pass	70' 00"	25' 05"	9' 00"
Emerald Empress	ES	1994	D	600 pass	150' 00"	33' 00"	9' 00"
Commuter	CF	1960	D	155 pass	64' 06"	33' 00"	9' 00"
Endeavor	CF	1987	D	150 pass	101' 00"	34' 06"	10' 00"
Kelley Islander	CF	1969	D	149 pass	100' 00"	34' 03"	8' 00"

PN-2 — NORTHUMBERLAND FERRIES LTD., CHARLOTTETOWN, PEI

Vessel	Type	Year	Eng	Cap	Length	Beam	Depth
Confederation	CF	1962	D	2,370	285' 04"	62' 00"	20' 01"
Lord Selkirk	CF	1958	D	1,834	260' 07"	54' 07"	18' 01"
Prince Edward	CF	1972	D	1,772	250' 04"	55' 04"	18' 01"
Prince Nova	CF	1964	D	1,765	250' 01"	55' 04"	18' 01"

PO-1 — ONTARIO MINISTRY OF TRANS. & COMMUNICATION, KINGSTON, ON

Vessel	Type	Year	Eng	Cap	Length	Beam	Depth
Amherst islander	CF	1955	D	125 pass	106' 00"	38' 00"	10' 00"
Frontenac II	CF	1962	D	300 pass	181' 00"	45' 00"	10' 00"
Glenora	CF	1952	D	122 pass	127' 00"	33' 00"	9' 00"
The Quinte Loyalist	CF	1954	D	122 pass	127' 00"	32' 00"	8' 00"
Wolfe Islander III	CF	1975	D	338 pass	205' 00"	68' 00"	6' 00"

PO-2 — ONTARIO NORTHLAND TRANS. COMMISSION, OWEN SOUND, ON

Vessel	Type	Year	Eng	Cap	Length	Beam	Depth
Chi-Cheemaun	CF	1974	D	530 pass	365' 05"	61' 00"	21' 00"
Nindawayma	CF	1976	D	400 pass	333' 06"	55' 00"	36' 06"

(Monte Cruceta '76 - '76, Monte Castillo '76 - '78, Manx Viking '78 - '87, Manx '87 - '87, Skudenes '87 - '89, Ontario No.1 '89 - '89)
(Last operated in 1992 — Currently laid up in Owen Sound, ON)

PP-1 — PARKER BOAT LINE, INC., PUT-IN-BAY, OH

Vessel	Type	Year	Eng	Cap	Length	Beam	Depth
Erie Isle	CF	1951	D	189 pass	72' 00"	24' 00"	8' 00"
Yankee Clipper	CF	1952	D	299 pass	70' 00"	24' 00"	8' 00"

PP-2 — PELEE ISLAND TRANSPORTATION SERVICES, PELEE ISLAND, ON

Vessel	Type	Year	Eng	Cap	Length	Beam	Depth
Jiimaan	CF	1992	D	400 pass	176' 09"	42' 03"	13' 06"
Pelee Islander	CF	1960	D	268 pass	145' 00"	32' 00"	10' 00"
Upper Canada	CF	1949	D	80 pass	143' 00"	36' 03"	11' 04"

PP-3 — PICTURED ROCKS CRUISES, INC., MUNISING, MI

Vessel	Type	Year	Eng	Cap	Length	Beam	Depth
Grand Island	ES	1989	D	202 pass	68' 00"	16' 01"	5' 01"
Miners Castle	ES	1974	D	204 pass	68' 00"	17' 00"	5' 00"
Miss Munising	ES	1967	D	131 pass	60' 00"	14' 00"	4' 04"
Miss Superior	ES	1984	D	204 pass	68' 00"	17' 00"	5' 00"
Pictured Rocks	ES	1972	D	130 pass	60' 00"	14' 00"	4' 04"

PP-4 — PLAUNT TRANSPORTATION, CHEYBOGAN, MI

Vessel	Type	Year	Eng	Cap	Length	Beam	Depth
Kristen D.	CF	1988	D	80 pass	64' 11"	36' 00"	6' 05"

PP5 — PMCL BOAT CRUISES, MIDLAND, ON

Vessel	Type	Year	Eng	Cap	Length	Beam	Depth
Island Queen IV	ES		D	60 pass			
Miss Midland	ES	1974	D	250 pass	68' 07"	19' 04"	6' 04"
Ste. Marie I	ES		D	72 pass			

Fleet No. and Name Vessel Name	Year Built	Type of Ship	Type of Engine	Cargo Cap. or Gross*	Length	Beam	Depth or Draft*
PP-6 — PORT CITY PRINCESS, INC., NORTH MUSKEGON, MI							
Port City Princess	ES	1966	D	208 pass	64' 09"	30' 00"	5' 06"
PP-7 — THE PUT-IN-BAY BOAT LINE, PUT-IN-BAY, OH							
Jet Express	PF	1989	D	385 pass	93' 00"	28' 05"	8' 04"
Jet Express II	PF	1992	D	395 pass	96' 00"	28' 06"	3' 06"
PR-1 — PRIDE OF WINDSOR CRUISE LINES, WINDSOR, ON							
Stella Borealis	ES	1989	D	275 pass	130 '00"		7' 00"
PR-2 — RUSSEL ISLAND TRANSIT CO., ALGONAC, MI							
Islander	CF	1982	D	49 pass	41' 00"	15' 00"	3' 06"
PS-1 — ST. LAWRENCE CRUISE LINES, INC., KINGSTON, ON							
Canadian Empress	PA	1981	D	66 pass	104' 00"	30' 00"	8' 00"
PS-2 — SANDUSKY BOAT LINE, SANDUSKY, OH							
City of Sandusky	ES	1987	D	299 pass	110' 00"	26' 00"	6' 00"
PS-3 — SHEPLER'S MACKINAC ISLAND FERRY SERVICE, MACKINAW CITY, MI							
Capt. Shepler	PF	1986	D	265 pass	78' 00"	21' 00"	3' 00"
Felicity	PF	1972	D	150 pass	65' 00"	18' 00"	3' 00"
Hope	PF	1975	D	150 pass	65' 00"	18' 00"	3' 00"
Sacre Bleu	PK	1959	D	150 pass	64' 09"	32' 09"	9' 09"
PS-4 — SHORELINE MARINE CO., CHICAGO, IL							
Marlyn	ES	1961	D	300 pass	65' 00"	25' 00"	7' 00"
Shoreline	ES	1953	D	300 pass	61' 07"	16' 00"	4' 05"
PS-5 - SOCIETE DES TRAVERSIERS DU QUEBEC, QUEBEC, PQ							
Jos. Deschenes	CF	1980	D	400 pass	190' 00"	71' 00"	15' 00"
Catherine LeGardeur	CF	1974	D	6,122	312' 05"	63' 00"	39' 02"
Lomer Gouin	CF	1971	D	70 pass	214' 00"	71' 06"	11' 06"
Armand Imbeau	CF	1980	D	400 pass	190' 00"	71' 00"	15' 00"
Grues Des Iles	CF	1981	D	120 PASS.	101' 02"	39' 06"	12' 05"
Alphonse des Jarnins	CF	1971	D	70 pass	214' 00"	71' 06"	11' 06"
Lucien L.	CF	1967	D	300 pass	222' 00"	62' 00"	15' 05"
Camille Marcoux	CF	1974	D	600 pass	310' 00"	60' 06"	16' 00"
Radisson	CF	1954	D	1,043	164' 03"	72' 00"	10' 06"
Joseph Savard	CF	1985	D	1,445	207' 02"	72' 02"	18' 00"
Trois Rivieres	CF	1962	D	600 pass	200' 00"	70' 06"	10' 00"
PS-6 — SOO LOCKS BOAT TOURS, SAULT STE. MARIE, MI							
AMERICAN AND CANADIAN LOCK TOURS							
Bide-A-Wee	ES	1955	D	272 pass	64' 07"	25' 00"	6' 05"
Hiawatha	ES	1959	D	272 pass	64' 07"	25' 00"	6' 05"
Holiday	ES	1957	D	272 pass	64' 07"	25' 00"	6' 05"
FAMOUS SOO LOCKS CRUISES							
LeVoyageur	ES	1959	D	294 pass	65' 00"	25' 00"	7' 00"
Nokomis	ES	1959	D	283 pass	65' 00"	25' 00"	7' 00"

Roger LeLievre

Toronto ferry William Inglis celebrated her 60th birthday in 1995.

Fleet No. and Name Vessel Name	Year Built	Type of Ship	Type of Engine	Cargo Cap. or Gross*	Length	Beam	Depth or Draft*

PS-7 — SPECIALTY RESTAURANTS CORP, ANAHEIM, CA

Lansdowne	RT	1884	B	1,571*	319' 00"	41' 03"	13' 00"

(Last operated in 1974 — Currently laid up in Lorain, OH)

PS-8 — STAR LINE MACKINAC ISLAND FERRY, ST. IGNACE, MI

Cadillac	PF	1990	D	150 pass	64' 07"	22' 00"	5' 00"
Joliet	PF	1993	D	150 pass	64' 07"	22' 00"	5' 00"
La Salle	PF	1983	D	150 pass	64' 00"	22' 00"	5' 00"
Marquette	PF	1979	D	150 pass	64' 00"	22' 00"	5' 00"
Nicolet	PF	1985	D	150 pass	61' 00"	22' 00"	5' 00"
Radisson	PF	1988	D	350 pass	83' 00"	24' 00"	5' 00"

PS-9— STEAMER COLUMBIA FOUNDATION, DETROIT, MI

Columbia	ES	1902	R	2,566 pass	216' 00"	60' 00"	13' 06"

(Last operated September 2, 1991 — Currently laid up in Ecorse, MI)

PS-10— STEAMER STE. CLAIRE FOUNDATION, DETROIT, MI

Ste. Claire	ES	1910	R	2,416 pass	197' 00"	65' 00"	14' 00"

(Last operated September 2, 1991 — Currently laid up in Ecorse, MI)

PT-1— TORONTO METROPOLITAN PARK DEPT., TORONTO, ON

William Inglis	PF	1935	D	250 pass	101' 00"	25' 00"	10' 00"
Sam McBride	PF	1939	D	475 pass	126' 00"	33' 00"	10' 00"
Thomas Rennie	PF	1951	D	400 pass	126' 00"	33' 00"	10' 00"
Ongiara	PF	1963	D	200 pass	78' 00"	36' 00"	8' 00"
Trillium	PF	1919	D	500 pass	150' 00"	30' 00"	8' 04"

PT-2 — TRAVERSE TALL SHIP CO., TRAVERSE CITY, MI

Malabar	PA	1975	SAIL	52 pass	105' 00"	20' 00"	8' 00"
Manitou	PA	1983	SAIL	68 pass	114' 00"	21' 00"	9' 00"

PU-1 — UNCLE SAM BOAT TOURS, INC., ALEXANDRIA BAY, NY

Alexandria Belle	ES	1964	D	310 pass	65' 00"	22' 00"	10' 00"
Island Wanderer	ES	1973	D	225 pass	64' 05"	17' 00"	6' 04"
Miss Clayton III	ES		D	250 pass	245' 00"	22' 00"	
Miss Clayton IV	ES		D	136 pass	64' 00"	18' 00"	
Uncle Sam	ES	1916	D	76 pass	54' 00"	10' 00"	3' 10"
Uncle Sam VI	ES	1924	D	60 pass	64' 00"	18' 00"	2' 06"
Uncle Sam VII	ES	1958	D	270 pass	63' 00"	18' 00"	15' 03"

PU-2 — U.S. NATIONAL PARK SERVICE, ISLE ROYALE NAT. PARK, HOUGHTON, MI

Charlie Mott	PF	1953	D	28*	56' 00"	14' 00"	4' 07"
Ranger III	PF	1958	D	140 pass	165' 00"	34' 00"	15' 03"
J. E. Colombe	TB	1953	D	25*	45' 00"	12' 05"	5' 03"
Beaver	BC	1952	B	550	110' 00"	32' 00"	6' 05"
Greenstone	TK	1977	B	30 bbls	81' 00"	24' 00"	6' 01"

PU-3 — UPPER CANADA STEAMBOATS, INC., BROCKVILLE, ON

Miss Brockville	ES		D	42 pass	48' 00"	10' 00"	4' 00"
Miss Brockville IV	ES		D	21 pass	45' 00"	10' 00"	5' 00"
Miss Brockville V	ES		D	45 pass	62' 00"	13' 00"	5' 00"
Miss Brockville VI	ES		D	5 pass	38' 00"	8' 00"	3' 00"

Fleet No. and Name Vessel Name	Type of Ship	Year Built	Type of Engine	Cargo Cap. or Gross*	Length	Beam	Depth or Draft*
Miss Brockville VI	ES		D	5 pass	38' 00"	8' 00"	3' 00"
Miss Brockville VII	ES		D	60 pass	66' 00"	15' 00"	5' 00"
Miss Brockville VIII	ES		D	32 pass	48' 00"	12' 00"	5' 00"

PV-1 — VISTA FLEET, DULUTH, MN
Vista King	ES	1978	D	265 pass	78' 00"	23' 00"	5' 02"
Vista Star	ES	1987	D	300 pass	91' 00"	26' 00"	5' 02"

PV-2 — VOIGHT'S MARINE SERVICES, GILLS ROCK, WI
Bounty	ES	1968	D	51 pass	40' 00"	14' 00"	3' 03"
Island Clipper	ES	1987	D	149 pass	65' 00"	20' 00"	5' 00"
Yankee Clipper	ES	1971	D	103 pass	54' 00"	17' 00"	5' 00"

PW-1 — WAGNER CHARTER CO., INC., CHICAGO, IL
Trinidad	ES	1926	D	150 pass	100' 00"	23' 00"	9' 00"

PW-2 — WALPOLE - ALGONAC FERRY LINE, PORT LAMBTON, ON
City of Algonac	CF	1990	D	250 pass	80' 04"	26' 01"	6' 09"
Lowell D.	CF	1946	D	30 pass	48' 07"	17' 06"	5' 02"
Walpole Islander	CF	1986	D	100 pass	74' 00"	33' 00"	7' 00"

PW-3 - WASHINGTON ISLAND FERRY LINE, INC., WASHINGTON ISLAND, WI
Eyrarbakki	CF	1970	D	150 pass	87' 00"	36' 00"	7' 06"
Robert Noble	CF	1979	D	175 pass	90' 04"	36' 00"	8' 03"
C. G. Richter	CF	1950	D	100 pass	70' 06"	25' 00"	9' 05"
Voyager	CF	1960	D	150 pass	65' 00"	35' 00"	8' 00"
Washington	CF	1989	D	250 pass	100' 00"	37' 00"	6' 05"

PW-4 — WENDELLA SIGHTSEEING CO., CHICAGO, IL
Queen of Andersonville	ES	1962	D	38 pass	40' 00"	5' 00"	3' 05"
Wendella Clipper	ES	1958	D	140 pass	67' 00"	20' 00"	4' 00"
Wendella Limited	ES	1992	D	150 pass	68' 00"	20' 00"	4' 09"
Wendella Sunliner	ES	1961	D	108 pass	68' 00"	17' 00"	5' 00"

Philip A. Clayton

Former Bob-Lo passenger boats Columbia and Ste. Claire laid-up at Ecorse, 2 December, 1995.

Saltie Oak loads general cargo at Erie during July, 1995.

LeLievre

OVERSEAS VESSELS ON THE LAKES & SEAWAY, 1995

Compiled by **Albert G. Ballert, Great Lakes Commission, Ann Arbor, MI.**

Note: Data is based on the daily transit reports for the U. S. Seaway locks and from supplemental port cargo data. The dates are for the westbound passages through the Eisenhower Lock. LOA and Beam are the vessel's overall length and beam in feet. (T) is for tankers. 1995 saw 220 vessels from 34 different countries make 438 trips into the St. Lawrence Seaway and Great Lakes distinguishing 1995 as the fifth lowest year for overseas vessel traffic in the past 16 years.

Flags of Registry

AB	Antigua / Barbuda	HK	Hong Kong	PH	Philippines
BA	Bahamas	IN	India	PO	Poland
CA	Canada	IT	Italy	RO	Romania
CH	Peoples Rep. of China	LI	Liberia	RU	Russia
CR	Croatia	LT	Lithuania	SI	Singapore
CU	Cuba	MA	Malaysia	SP	Spain
CY	Cyrpus	MI	Marshall Islands	SV	St. Vincent/
DE	Denmark	MT	Malta		Grenadines
DU	Netherlands	MY	Myanmar	TH	Thailand
ES	Estonia	NA	Netherland Antilles	TU	Turkey
FI	Finland	NO	Norway	VA	Vanuatu
GK	Greece			YU	Yugoslavia

1995 Westbound Transits:

March/April-59; **May**-52 **June**-40; **July**-49; **August**- 39; **September**- 51; **October**-58; **November**-70; **December**-20; *Season total* - 438

Westbound Transits through December 1980 - 1994

1994-588; **1993**-427; **1992**-399; **1991**-429; **1990**- 437; **1989**-533; **1988**-745;**1987**-572; **1986**-663; **1985**-581; **1984**-703; **1983**-679; **1982**- 815; **1981**-755; **1980**-918

In addition to the overseas cargo vessels listed, the ***Caribbean Mercy*** (PA), a hospital aid and supply ship, entered the lakes on 5/11 and made tour calls at a number of ports before departing about 9/20.

Name Changes: *Kapitonas Gudin* (4/24 and 7/1) became *Kapitonas Kaminskas* (11/3) and *Stellanova* (4/29) became *Gajah Borneo* (12/8).

Con't on Page 82

Vessel Name	Flag	LOA	Beam	Year Blt.	1st	2nd	3rd	4th	5th	6th	7th
Aivik	CA	360	61	1980	3/21	6/2					
Alam Senang	MA	585	76	1984	5/7	7/4	11/1				
Alam United	MA	585	76	1984	4/15						
Alidon	CY	275			11/2						
Alpha	LI	580	75	1976	5/4	9/12	11/19				
Altair	AB	322			10/21						
An Ze Jiang	CH	491			9/12						
Anna	CY	601	75	1976	6/10	11/10					
Antalina	CY	585	76	1984	4/25						
APJ Anjli	IN	577	76	1982	5/31						
Aptmariner	LI	619	76	1979	5/4	8/5	10/1	11/20			
Aquarius	IT	397	59	1978	12/12						
Areito	CU	486			11/17						
Argut	UK	312			9/1						
Arma	MT	473			4/30	9/28					
Arosa	CY	626	75	1975	11/10						
Asia Trader	PA	591			9/7	11/4					
Aslan I	TU	396			9/6	12/9					
Astra Lift	BA	307			8/3	10/17					
Atlanta Forest	MT	522	69	1978	5/6						
Atlantis Spirit	CY	498	75	1977	4/15						
Aurora Topaz	LI	640			5/21	7/22	9/27	11/17			
Avdeevka	UK	571			10/7	11/23					
Aynur Kalkavan	TU	583			10/29						
Barbara E	SP	336			8/30						
Barbara H	CY	622	75	1976	8/24	10/23					
Beluga	MT	585	74	1977	10/26						
Bergon	SW	331	54	1978	7/27						
Beta Luck	GK	559			9/27						
Blue Bill	CY	621			8/7	11/2					
Bontegracht	DU	263			11/12						
C. Martin	MT	538			5/13						
Calliroe Patronicola	GK	600	76	1985	10/11		12/7				
Capetan Michalis	GK	593	76	1981	8/2						
Chada Naree	TH	479			5/25						
Ciovo	PA	479	73	1977	9/3						
Concorde (T)	SV	320			7/3	8/18	11/24				
Cvijeta Zuzoric	YU	599	74	1974	9/26						
Darya Kamal	HK	617	76	1983	4/23	6/3	7/28	10/22			
Dmitriy Donskoy	RU	532			5/5						
Dmitriy Pozharskiy	RU	532			4/15						
Docegulf	LI	674	76	1979	10/22						
Edda	AB	323			5/27						
Eemshorn	DU	294			5/7						
El Kef	LI	600			10/22						
Elikon	BA	582	75	1980	4/14						
Erikousa Wave	CY	601	74	1986	11/10						
Evmar	CY	593	76	1976	4/30	10/9					
Federal Aalesund	NO	590	76	1985	8/19						
Federal Agno	PH	600	76	1985	4/28	7/14	10/9				
Federal Bergen	NO	593	76	1984	10/31						

Hercegovina is eastbound in the Welland Canal, 17 July 1995.

Roger LeLievre

Vessel Name	Flag	LOA	Beam	Year Blt.	1st	2nd	3rd	4th	5th	6th	7th
Federal Calliope	LI	623	76	1978	4/22	7/16	8/30				
Federal Dora	GK	623	76	1978	6/20	8/13	10/10				
Federal Fraser	PH	730	76	1983	3/27	5/18	11/17				
Federal Fuji	LI	598	76	1986	5/25	10/10					
Federal Inger	NO	593	76	1978	9/23						
Federal MacKenzie	HK	730	76	1983	4/19	6/8	7/29	10/11	12/3		
Federal Manitou	NO	585	76	1983	4/20	9/8					
Federal Matane	NO	585	76	1984	3/28	6/6	10/11				
Federal Nord	NO	591	76	1981	7/31						
Federal Oslo	NO	601	76	1985	5/19	8/3	9/22	11/5			
Federal Polaris	JA	600	76	1985	4/3	7/15	8/29	11/3			
Federal Vibeke	NO	618	76	1981	7/2	10/28					
Federal Vigra	NO	590	76	1985	6/7	7/17					
Finnfighter	FI	522			8/18						
Finnsnes	PA	441	68	1979	10/8						
Fjordnes	NO	490			10/15						
Freja Nordic (T)	BA	407			9/17						
Frines	PA	441	68	1978	12/1						
Fujisan Maru	TH	481			10/17						
Furunes	PA	441	68	1979	4/21						
Gajah Borneo	MA	327			12/8						
General Cabal	PH	477			4/2	5/15	7/24	9/16	11/7		
George L.	GK	597	75	1975	8/26						
Golden Shield	PA	417	66	1982	5/19						
Golden Sky	CY	626	75	1975	4/20	8/2	9/20	11/28			
Great Laker	MY	591	76	1987	5/22	11/28					
Gunay-A	TU	617	76	1981	4/12	6/10	7/29	10/13			
Haight	BA	581			10/10						
Handy Laker	PH	585	76	1984	4/30	10/6					
Handymariner	LI	619	76	1978	5/26	7/24	9/19				
Hercegovina	MT	645	75	1977	4/15	6/29	9/6	11/7			
Hilal-II	TU	585	76	1981	7/18						
Holck-Larsen	IN	628	75	1981	4/5	12/12					
Hope I	MT	617	76	1982	4/14						
Hydra	BA	568	75	1977	8/18	10/19					
Icepurha (T)	BA	619	72	1968	4/26	6/25					
Ikan Selayang	SI	590	76	1981	10/2						
Indian Express	VA	509			8/2						
Island Gem	GK	585	76	1984	9/10	11/25					
Island Skipper	GK	585	76	1984	3/30	6/7	9/5	11/21			
Ivi	LI	591	76	1979	7/8	11/11					
Jeannie	GK	601	75	1977	12/2						
Jing Hong Hai	CH	594			11/16						
Jo Hassel	SV	356			5/5						
Jo Palm	DU	378			10/23						
Kapitan Zamyatin	RU	498	69	1976	5/26						
Kapitonas A. Lucka	LT	480	68	1980	5/9	8/23	11/5				
Kapitonas Dubinin	LT	480	68	1979	6/22	8/7	11/4				
Kapitonas Gudin	LT	480	68	1978	4/25	7/1					
Kapitonas Izmiakov	LT	480	68	1977	4/20						
Kapitonas Kaminskas	LT	480	68	1978	11/3						

Roger LeLievre

Utviken visits Hamilton, 1 October, 1995.

Vessel Name	Flag	LOA	Beam	Year Blt.	1st	2nd	3rd	4th	5th	6th	7th
Kapitonas Mesceriakov	LT	480	68	1978	7/9	9/16	11/28				
Kapitonas Reutov	LT	480	68	1976	4/10	6/7		7/23	10/4	11/25	
Kapitonas Stulpinas	LT	480	68	1981	10/4						
Kapitonas Vavilov	LT	480	68	1979	6/11						
Karen D.	CY	386			9/6						
Kirby D.	CY	386			5/8						
Kobuleti (T)	MT	496			6/17						
Konstantis F.	GK	472			5/18						
Lake Carling	MI	591	76	1992	7/12	10/31					
Lake Challenger	PA	591	76	1985	5/6	7/17	10/8				
Lake Champlain	MI	591	76	1992	5/18	7/3	8/17	10/7	12/2		
Lake Charles	MI	591	76	1990	7/18	9/24	11/14				
Lake Erie	MI	734	77	1980	4/7	7/13	9/5	10/23			
Lake Michigan	CY	730	77	1981	4/28	6/17	9/6	10/17	12/8		
Lake Ontario	MI	734	77	1980	3/25	5/12	8/15	12/11			
Lake Superior	CY	734	77	1981	3/26	9/13					
Lake Tahoe	MI	608	75	1973	7/22						
Laserbeam	MT	600	73	1974	10/13						
Liberty Sky	PA	585	76	1985	10/17						
Lida	CY	214			6/22						
LT Argosy	IN	607	76	1984	3/25	6/1	11/13				
LT Odyssey	IN	607	76	1984	11/30						
Luckyman	CY	585	76	1980	5/28	7/28	10/6	11/18			
Luna Verde	PH	592	76	1986	5/2	9/26					
M. Hass	BA	532	74	1977	4/16	5/26					
Maisi	CU	486			11/28						
Makeevka	RU	645	76	1982	11/12						
Malinska	MT	730	76	1987	4/30	9/30	11/21				
Margaret John	MT	379	57	1977	4/19	7/4					
Maria S. J.	GK	597			4/22						
Marilis T.	CY	585	76	1984	11/28						
Marka L.	GK	597	75	1975	4/22						
Mikhail Kutuzov	RU	532			5/24						
Milin Kamak	BU	608	75	1979	11/26						
Mljet	MT	622	75	1983	5/9	9/26					
Moutain Blossom (T)	BA	528	75	1986	11/2	12/9					
Nea Doxa	GK	617	76	1984	5/20	7/6	11/16				
Necat-A	TU	656	76	1981	6/29	11/27					
Nomadic Patria	NO	512			6/16						
Nordic Blossom (T)	LI	505	75	1981	9/3	11/13					
Nyanza	BA	498			10/14						
Oak	BA	509			7/2	8/29	11/15				
Ocean Priti	PA	599	75	1982	9/6						
Odranes	BA	471	68	1992	6/7	9/12					
Olympic Mentor	GK	600	76	1984	7/7	8/28	11/30				
Olympic Merit	GK	600	76	1984	9/9						
Olympic Miracle	GK	600	76	1984	4/13	6/7	8/6				
Omisalj	MT	729	76	1987	3/27	5/22	7/13	11/27			
Pantazis L.	GK	597	75	1974	4/29	6/25					
Parkgracht	DU	349			6/11						
Peonia	LI	648	76	1983	5/18	10/11					

Vessel Name		Flag	LOA	Beam	Year Blt.	1st	2nd	3rd	4th	5th	6th	7th
Petka		MT	729	76	1986	4/1	5/28	9/10	11/19			
Phoenix M		CY	581	75	1976	11/16						
Polydefkis		GK	622	75	1976	8/2	10/18					
Pomorze Zachodnie		PO	591	76	1985	5/17	9/2					
Pontokratis		GK	590	76	1981	4/26	11/2					
Pontoporos		GK	581	75	1984	7/6	11/23					
Praxitelis		GK	621			9/10	11/16					
Pride of Donegal		LI	518			12/9						
Project Europa		NA	456	75	1983	10/19						
Proof Trader	(T)	NO	318	40	1975	11/8						
Punica		LI	648	76	1983	6/26	8/16	10/26				
Rantum	(T)	CY	346			9/24	10/6					
Razboient		RO	521			7/2						
Rhea		GK	593	76	1978	5/24	9/16	11/23				
Riomar		CY	445			9/24						
Romo Maersk	(T)	DE	558			7/16	8/6	12/12				
Rong Jiang		CH	463			11/20						
Rose Island		PA	472			10/26						
Rubin Eagle		PH	486			11/15						
Ruder Boskovic		YU	599	74	1974	9/23	11/18					
Sac Malaga		PA	626	75	1976	5/31	8/14					
Saskatchewan Pioneer		BA	730	76	1983	4/27	6/29	8/28	11/3			
Sea Monarch		MT	640	76	1984	8/9	10/17					
Seadaniel		PA	581	75	1976	5/19						
Seapearl II		MT	581			4/12						
Sidsel Knutsen	(T)	NO	533	76	1993	6/13	8/9	10/1	11/15			
Solta		MT	626	75	1984	9/16	11/9					
Soren Toubro		IN	628	75	1981	4/26	6/12	10/11				
South Islands		CY	472			10/31						
Staalvang		NO	251			7/29						
Staberg		NO	600			4/21						
Steel Flower		PA	730	76	1977	6/7	8/12	11/2				
Stellamare		NA	289	51	1982	5/14						
Stellanova		NA	327			4/29						
Stepan Razin		RU	532			5/5						
Stevnsland		AB	290			9/17						
Stolt Alliance	(T)	PA	405	66	1985	4/24	6/2	7/12	8/28	10/5	11/23	
Stolt Aspiration	(T)	PA	423	66	1987	4/5	5/14	6/23	8/10	9/18	10/30	12/3
Stolt Taurus	(T)	LI	405	66	1986	11/28						
Stormy Annie		PA	522			11/26						
Storon		SW	470	61	1975	6/2						
Sunny Blossom	(T)	BA	528	75	1986	5/7						
Super Vision		PH	400	66	1986	5/18						
Thor I		LI	542	75	1978	4/16	6/29	9/3	11/11			
Thorscape		SI	542	75	1977	5/10	7/15	9/27	12/1			
Tim Buck		RU	532			5/20						
Titan Scan		NA	405			8/31						
Trans Arctic	(T)	NO	383	57	1991	5/8	6/12	7/17				
Trias		GK	730	76	1977	7/17	9/1	10/18				
Turid Knutsen	(T)	NO	533	76	1993	4/7	5/19	7/13	9/8		10/22	12/8

Vessel Name	Flag	LOA	Beam	Year Blt.	1st	2nd	3rd	4th	5th	6th	7th
Turkay B.	TU	387			6/26						
Ulloa	SI	585	76	1983	4/13	8/29	10/31				
Union	HK	585	76	1984	7/14						
Utviken	BA	621			4/14	6/6	8/15	9/28	11/21		
Uznadze	MT	496			12/16						
Varjakka	FI	522			10/28						
Vasiliy Musinskiy	RU	498	69	1974	6/18						
Vekua	MT	496			6/14	7/31	9/21				
Viljandi	ES	458	63	1978	5/18	6/24					
Vulcan	CY	626	75	1975	4/13	7/9	11/15				
Wana Naree	TH	576			7/11						
Winter Star	CY	580	76	1978	5/14	10/18	12/9				
Ziemia Chelminska	PO	591	76	1984	5/5	7/1	9/14	11/20			
Ziemia Gnieznienska	PO	591	76	1985	3/30	6/7	8/4	11/10			
Ziemia Suwalska	PO	591	76	1984	4/4	7/8	10/2	11/28			
Ziemia Tarnowska	PO	591	76	1985	4/22	7/22	10/21				
Ziemia Zamojska	PO	591	76	1984	4/13	6/22	8/28	10/27			

Port Huron pilot boat meets the Indian-flag Soren Toubro.

Neil Schultheiss

Saltwater vessel makes an early spring entry at Duluth-Superior harbor.

Jerry Bielicki

104

Roger LeLievre
Coast Guard cutter Biscayne Bay nears her base at Sault Ste. Marie, MI.

EXTRA TONNAGE ...

Cartierdoc in the St. Lawrence River.   Bryan C. Wood-Thomas

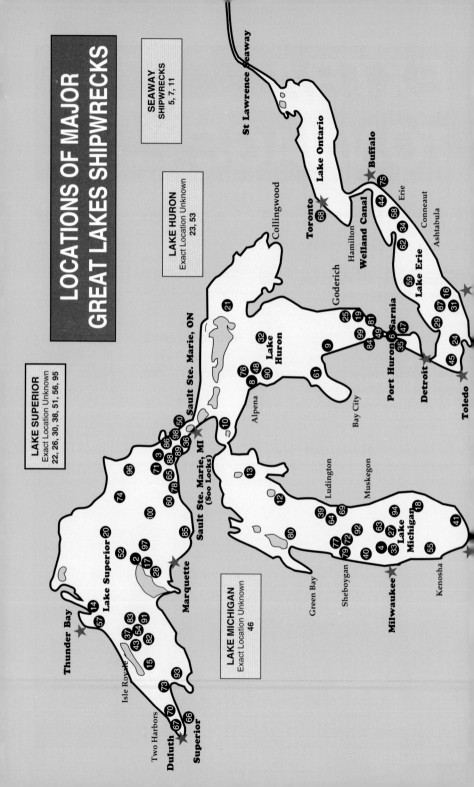

SHIPWRECK KEY

The first 15 shipwrecks are listed chronologically; the remainder alphabetically. Listing includes only those vessels declared a total loss ... those salvaged and returned to service are not listed. Please match the shipwreck's number to its location on the map on previous page (locations are approximate). Casualties, where known, are listed after reason lost (no entry means no lives known lost). An asterisk indicates the ship was lost in the Great Storm of Nov. 11-13, 1913, which claimed 11 major vessels and took more than 250 lives.

Vessel	Date lost	Reason lost, location, # of casualties
1. **Jupiter**	9-1990	Exploded, burned at Bay City (1 lost)
2. **Mesquite (WLB-305)**	12-1989	Stranded, (later sunk as underwater preserve) off the Keweenaw Peninsula
3. **Edmund Fitzgerald**	11-1975	Foundered, cause unknown, on Lake Superior (29 lost)
4. **Jennifer**	12-1974	Foundered, heavy seas, off Milwaukee
5. **Roy A. Jodrey**	11-1974	Hit obstruction, sank, in St. Lawrence Seaway
6. **Sidney E. Smith Jr.**	06-1972	In collision with Str. Parker Evans at Port Huron
7. **Eastcliffe Hall**	07-1970	Hit obstruction, sank in St. Lawrence River (9 lost)
8. **Nordmeer**	11-1966	Stranded in gale *(superstructure still visible)* off Alpena
9. **Daniel J. Morrell**	11-1966	Foundered, heavy seas, off Harbor Beach (28 lost)
10. **Cedarville**	05-1965	Hit in fog by M/V Topdalsfjord in Straits of Mackinac (10 lost)
11. **Leecliffe Hall**	09-1964	Collision with M/V Appolonia, St. Lawrence River (3 lost)
12. **Francisco Morazon**	11-1960	Stranded *(much of wreck still visible)* on S. Manitou Island
13. **Carl D. Bradley**	11-1958	Foundered in gale near Beaver Island (33 lost)
14. **Scotiadoc**	06-1953	Hit in fog by Str. Burlington off Thunder Bay (1 lost)
15. **Henry Steinbrenner**	05-1953	Foundered in heavy seas off Isle Royale (17 lost)
16. **Admiral** (tug)	12-1942	Foundered in heavy seas off Cleveland (7 lost)
17. **Altadoc**	12-1927	Stranded, Keweenaw Point , Lake Superior
18. **Andaste**	09-1929	Foundered, Lake Michigan (25 lost)
19. **Argus***	11-1913	Foundered, Lake Huron (25 lost)
20. **Arlington**	05-1940	Foundered, Lake Superior (1 lost)
21. **Asia**	09-1882	Foundered, Georgian Bay (123 lost)
22. **Bannockburn**	11-1902	Disappeared on Lake Superior (21 lost)
23. **Kate L. Bruce**	11-1877	Disappered on Lake Huron (8 lost)
24. **Marshall F. Butters**	10-1916	Foundered in heavy seas in Lake Erie
25. **James Carruthers***	11-1913	Foundered in heavy seas in Lake Huron (25 lost)
26. **Cerisoler** (minesweeper)	11-1918	Disappeared on Lake Superior on maiden voyage (39 lost)
27. **Chicora**	01-1895	Disappeared in heavy seas on Lake Michigan (24 lost)
28. **City of Bangor**	11-1926	Stranded, Keweenaw Point, Lake Superior
29. **Clarion**	12-1909	Stranded, burned on Lake Erie. (15 lost, approx.)
30. **D.M. Clemson**	11-1908	Disappeared, Lake Superior (24 lost)
31. **Cleveco** (barge)	12-1942	Foundered in heavy seas, Lake Erie (11 lost)
32. **Clifton**	09-1924	Foundered in heavy seas, Lake Huron (27 lost)
33. **Dewitt Clinton**	10-1839	Sank off Milwaukee (5 lost)
34. **James B. Colgate**	10-1916	Foundered in heavy seas, Lake Erie (24 lost)
35. **Omar D. Conger**	04-1922	Exploded at Port Huron (4 lost)
36. **John B. Cowle**	07-1909	Hit in fog by Str. Issac M. Scott, Whitefish Bay (14 lost)
37. **George M. Cox**	05-1933	Stranded, sank off Isle Royale
38. **Cyprus**	09-1907	Foundered, heavy seas, Lake Superior (21 lost)

Con't on Page 94

Cont'd from Page 93

39. **William B. Davock** . . . . .11-1940 . . . . . .Foundered off Pentwater, Lake Michigan (33 lost)
40. **L.R. Doty** . . . . .10-1898 . . . . . .Sank in heavy seas, Lake Michigan (17 lost)
41. **David Dows** . . . . .11-1889 . . . . . .Lost in Lake Michigan gale
42. **Eastland** . . . . .07-1915 . . . . . .Capsized at Chicago pier (835 lost)
43. **Emperor** . . . . .06-1947 . . . . . .Ran aground, Canoe Rocks off Isle Royale (12 lost)
44. **Erie** . . . . .08-1841 . . . . . .Exploded and burned on namesake lake (175 lost)
45. **D.L. Filer** . . . . .10-1916 . . . . . .Sank in heavy seas in western Lake Erie (6 lost)
46. **W. H. Gilcher** . . . . .11-1892 . . . . . .Foundered in Lake Michigan gale (21 lost)
47. **Hamonic** . . . . .07-1945 . . . . . .Burned at Sarnia, Ont.
48. **D.R. Hanna** . . . . .05-1919 . . . . . .In collision with Str. Quincy A. Shaw off Alpena
49. **Hydrus*** . . . . .11-1913 . . . . . .Foundered in Lake Huron (28 lost)
50. **Independence** . . . . .11-1853 . . . . . .Exploded at the Soo (4 lost)
51. **Inkerman** (minesweeper) . . . .11-1918 . . . . . .Disappeared on Lake Superior (39 lost)
52. **Iosco** . . . . .09-1905 . . . . . .Sank in Lake Superior storm (19 lost)
53. **Kaliyuga** . . . . .10-1905 . . . . . .Vanished on Lake Huron (16 lost)
54. **Kamloops** . . . . .12-1927 . . . . . .Lost off Isle Royale in gale (22 lost)
55. **Lady Elgin** . . . . .09-1860 . . . . . .Sank after collision on Lake Michigan, (297 lost)
56. **Lambton** . . . . .04-1922 . . . . . .Lighthouse tender vanished on Lake Superior (22 lost)
57. **Leafield *** . . . . .11-1913 . . . . . .Grounded, sank on Lake Superior (18 lost)
58. **John B. Lyon** . . . . .09-1900 . . . . . .Lost in Lake Erie gale (11 lost)
59. **Marquette-Bessemer No. 2** . . .12-1909 . . . . . .Carferry vanished on Lake Erie (36 lost)
60. **Seldon E. Marvin** . . . . .11-1914 . . . . . .Sank in Lake Superior gale (all hands)
61. **John A. McGean*** . . . . .11-1913 . . . . . .Foundered in Lake Huron (28 lost)
62. **Merida** . . . . .10-1916 . . . . . .Foundered in Lake Erie during a gale (23 lost)
63. **Milwaukee** . . . . .10-1929 . . . . . .Carferry vanished on Lake Michigan (all hands lost)
64. **Anna C. Minch** . . . . .11-1940 . . . . . .Foundered in Lake Michigan gale (24 lost)
65. **Myron** . . . . .11-1919 . . . . . .Foundered off Whitefish Point (17 lost)
66. **Alex. Nimick** . . . . .09-1907 . . . . . .Hit shoal, sank near Duluth (6 lost)
67. **Benjamin Noble** . . . . .04-1914 . . . . . .Disappeared off Two Harbors (21 lost)
68. **Noronic** . . . . .09-1949 . . . . . .Burned at dock in Toronto (139 lost)
69. **Novadoc** . . . . .11-1940 . . . . . .Sank in a Lake Michigan gale off Pentwater (2 lost)
70. **Onoko** . . . . .09-1915 . . . . . .Exploded, sank on Lake Superior
71. **Orinoco** . . . . .05-1923 . . . . . .Foundered in heavy seas near the Soo (5 lost)
72. **Our Son** . . . . .09-1930 . . . . . .Schooner foundered in Lake Michigan gale
73. **Ira H. Owen** . . . . .11-1905 . . . . . .Foundered, Lake Superior (19 lost)
74. **John Owen** . . . . .11-1919 . . . . . .Foundered, Lake Superior (22 lost)
75. **William Peacock** . . . . .09-1830 . . . . . .Boiler blew up at Buffalo (casualties unknown)
76. **Pewabic** . . . . .08-1865 . . . . . .Collided with Str. Meteor off Alpena (75-100)
77. **Pere Marquette No. 18** . . . . . 09-1910 . . . . . .Swamped in Lake Michigan gale (25 lost)
78. **Anna M. Peterson** . . . . .11-1914 . . . . . .Lost in Lake Superior gale (9 lost)
79. **Phoenix** . . . . .11-1847 . . . . . .Burned off Sheboygan (200)
80. **Plymouth** (barge)* . . . . .11-1913 . . . . . .Foundered in Lake Michigan (9 lost)
81. **Charles S. Price*** . . . . .11-1913 . . . . . .Overcome by seas on Lake Huron (28 lost)
82. **Prindoc** . . . . .06-1943 . . . . . .Sank after collision with Str. Battleford off Isle Royale
83. **Quedoc** . . . . .12-1927 . . . . . .Foundered in Lake Superior blow
84. **Regina*** . . . . .11-1913 . . . . . .Foundered in Lake Huron gale
85. **H.E. Runnells** . . . . .11-1919 . . . . . .Grounded, broke up near Grand Marais
86. **Sagamore** . . . . .07-1901 . . . . . .Sank, Lake Superior, after collision (3 lost)
87. **Sand Merchant** . . . . .10-1936 . . . . . .Foundered near Cleveland (19 lost)
88. **Saturn** . . . . .11-1872 . . . . . .Went down in gale west of Whitefish Point (7 lost)
89. **William F. Sauber** . . . . .10-1903 . . . . . .Sank in storm near Manitou Island (1 lost)
90. **Issac M. Scott *** . . . . .11-1913 . . . . . .Foundered in high seas on Lake Huron (28 lost)
91. **Ferdinand Schlesinger** . . . . . .05-1919 . . . . . .Sank in heavy weather near Isle Royale

Str. MORRELL LOST 30 YEARS AGO

Lake Huron, Nov. 29, 1966

Tom Manse

Daniel J. Morrell, in an early '60s photo.

All afternoon the message went out over Channel 52, asking mariners to be on the lookout for the overdue steamer **Daniel J. Morrell**. By the end of that grim November day, however, it became apparent the Great Lakes had claimed another victim. The 1906-built ore and coal carrier broke in half in 25-foot seas, whipped by 60 mph winds, 26 miles north of Harbor Beach, off Michigan's Thumb area. No distress call was sent, and there was just one survivor from her 28-man crew. Experts later theorized that "metal fatigue" was responsible for the sinking. The Morrell's 60-year-old hull had simply become too brittle with age. Shortly thereafter a number of other older vessels were withdrawn from service after tests showed their hulls had also become brittle. In an interesting footnote, the Morrell's sistership, **Edward Y. Townsend,** withdrawn from service immediately after the storm when her master noticed a crack in her deck plates, broke in half and sank two years later while being towed to an overseas scrapyard.

BIGGEST BLOWS: Besides the **"Great Storm of 1913,"** three other major cataclysms have earned proper names for their power and devastation: The Nov. 30 **"1905 Blow,"** which particularly crippled shipping on Lake Superior; what became known as the **"Black Friday Storm"** of Oct. 20, 1916, which hit particularly hard on Lake Erie; and the Nov. 11,1940 **"Armistice Day Storm,"** which focused mainly on Lake Michigan.

---

*The author acknowledges the invaluable help of **"Shipwreck"** by David D. Swayze, Harbor House Publishers, in preparing this reference.*

BELLS TOLL for the FITZGERALD

A number of events - including much-publicized dives to the wreck site - marked the 20th anniversary of the sinking of the **Edmund Fitzgerald**, November 10, 1995.

Services at Detroit's historic Mariner's Church, where the bell tolled

Observances marked 20th anniversary of tragedy.

29 times in memory of each crewman lost on the ill-fated ore carrier, and an emotional ceremony at Whitefish Point on eastern Lake Superior near where the Fitzgerald went down, helped bring about a kind of ending for the families of those who were lost when the freighter sank with all hands. In July of last year, with the approval of families who lost relatives on the ship, divers retrieved the Edmund Fitzgerald's brass bell, now part of a permanent exhibit and memorial at the Great Lakes Shipwreck Museum located just 17 miles from the Fitzgerald's final resting place. Eventually, the museum hopes to raise enough money to erect a wing dedicated to the Fitzgerald.

Many observers, especially the families of those lost with the ship, hope that the final dive has been made to the site, more than 500 feet deep in cold Lake Superior. But there is no guarantee the ship will be left to rest in peace. Indeed, a dispute over proper display of the bell stirred tempers across the region most of this past winter.

© Jene D. Quiran, Great Lakes Shipwreck Historical Society

Cheryl Rozman, daughter of Fitzgerald watchman Ransom Cundy, touches the Fitzgerald's bell aboard the tug Anglian Lady in 1995.

Photo taken in 1994 shows the open pilot house door on the port side of the Edmund Fitzgerald. The mystery of how the door was opened remains. Visible in the foreground are the submersible Clelia's video camera, lights and manipulator arm.

BOATWATCHING MADE EASY

Fans of Great Lakes and St. Lawrence Seaway shipping have one advantage over their saltwater counterparts - plenty of gathering places at which to meet, swap stories and photograph their favorite vessels. Whether in port or underway, the objects of our attention are never too distant. Here's some information to help track that elusive vessel.

BY PHONE: Try calling these recorded messages to keep abreast of vessel movements.

COMPANY	PHONE #	COVERAGE
Boatwatcher's Hotline	218-722-6489	Superior,WI, Duluth, Two Harbors, Taconite Harbor and Silver Bay, MN
CSX Coal Docks/Torco Dock	419-697-2304	Toledo, OH arrivals
DMIR Ore Dock	218-628-4590	Duluth, MN arrivals
DMIR Ore Dock	218-834-8190	Two Harbors, MN arrivals
Inland Lakes Management	517-354-4400	ILM Fleet movements
Michigan Limestone Docks	517-734-2117	Rogers City / Cedarville, MI arrivals
Presque Isle Corp.	517-595-6611	Stoneport, MI arrivals
Soo Control	906-635-3224	Previous day's traffic - St. Mary's River
Superior Midwest Enegy Terminal	715-392-3737	Superior, WI arrivals
Thunder Bay Port Authority	807-345-1256	Thunder Bay, ON arrivals
USS Great Lakes Fleet	218-727-3392	USS Fleet movements
Welland Canal	905-688-6464	Vessel movements

ON THE RADIO: With an inexpensive VHF scanner, you can tune to ship-to-shore traffic, using the following guide:

Bridge to Bridge Communications	**Ch. 13** (156.650 Mhz)	Commercial vessels only
Calling / Distress ONLY	**Ch. 16** (156.800 Mhz)	Calling / Distress ONLY
Working Channel	**Ch. 06** (156.300 Mhz)	Commercial vessels only
Working Channel	**Ch. 08** (156.400 Mhz)	Commercial vessels only
Soo Warehouse	**Ch. 08** (156.400 Mhz)	Supply boat at Soo
Sarnia Traffic - Sector 1	**Ch. 11** (156.550 Mhz)	Detour Reef to Lake St. Clair Light
Sarnia Traffic - Sector 2	**Ch. 12** (156.600 Mhz)	Long Point Light to Lake St. Clair Light
Seaway Beauharnois - Sector 1	**Ch. 14** (156.700 Mhz)	Montreal to about mid-Lake St. Francis
Seaway Eisenhower - Sector 2	**Ch. 12** (156.600 Mhz)	Mid-Lake St. Francis to Bradford Island
Seaway Iroquois - Sector 3	**Ch. 11** (156.550 Mhz)	Bradford Island to Crossover Island
Seaway Clayton - Sector 4	**Ch. 13** (156.650 Mhz)	Crossover Island to mid-Lake Ontario
St. Lawrence River portion		
Seaway Sodus - Sector 4	**Ch. 13** (156.650 Mhz)	mid-Lake Ontario to Point Petre
Lake Ontario portion		

Seaway Newcastle - Sector 5	**Ch. 13** (156.650 Mhz)	Mid-Lake Ontario to Welland Canal
Seaway Welland - Sector 6	**Ch. 14** (156.700 Mhz)	Welland Canal
Seaway Long Point - Sector 7	**Ch. 11** (156.550 Mhz)	Welland Canal to Long Point Light
		Lake Erie
Soo Control	**Ch. 12** (156.600 Mhz)	
Soo Lockmaster (call WUD-31)	**Ch. 14** (156.700 Mhz)	St. Mary's River Traffic Service
United States Coast Guard	**Ch. 21** (157.050 Mhz)	
	Ch. 22 (157.100 Mhz)	
	Ch. 23 (157.150 Mhz)	
J. W. Westcott II	**Ch. 10** (156.500 Mhz)	U. S. Mailboat, Detroit, MI

ALL THE NEWS THAT FITS

To keep up with Great Lakes gossip, news and innuendo, especially in the off-season when the rumors of vessel changes *really* start to fly, try joining one or more of the marine societies around the lakes (send a stamped, self-addressed envelope to Marine Publishing Co. for a free list), or subscribe to *Great Lakes Log,* 221 Water St., Boyne City, MI. 49712. On-line? Try the usenet group "alt.great-lakes" to contact others with similar interests.

Todd L. Davidson

N.M. Paterson & Son's Mantadoc loads grain at Toledo.

TALKING LIGHTS

RANGE LIGHTS

MASTHEAD LIGHT (White)
Masthead light means a white light placed over the fore and aft centerline of the vessel showing an unbroken light over an arc of the horizon of 225 degrees and so fixed as to show the light from right ahead to 22.5 degrees abaft the beam on either side of the vessel.

ALL-ROUND LIGHT (White) All-round light means a light showing a light over an arc of the horizon of 360 degrees.

STERNLIGHT (White) Sternlight means a white light placed as nearly as practicable at the stern showing an unbroken light over an arc of the horizon of 135 degrees and so-fixed as to show the light 67.5 degrees from right aft on each side of the vessel.

SIDELIGHTS (Green/Red) Sidelight means a green light on the starboard side and a red light on the port side, each showing an unbroken light over an arc of the horizon of 112.5 degrees and so-fixed as to show the light from right ahead to 22.5 degrees abaft the beam on its respective side.

SIDELIGHTS

Starboard - GREEN
(Right)

Port - RED
(Left)
(Shown here but normally unseen from this angle)

WHISTLE LIGHTS

Most Great Lakes vessels carry a whistle light atop the foremast in addition to the masthead light. It is often the capital letter initial of the owner and is white. The light, an additional safety device, comes on when the whistle is blown, stays on for the duration of each blast, and can also be seen in the daytime. On the newer generation of "lakers" with all superstructure located aft, the whistle light is atop the after mast and is usually amber.

PASSING

Oncoming vessel is directing her course to the right (starboard) for a port to port passing.

"Bows on" - a collision course. Change course to the right (starboard) if possible.

Oncoming vessel is directing her course to the left (port) for a starboard to starboard passing.

As a vessel changes course, it will look as if her all-round light is swinging and her masthead light is standing still. This is literally correct, as it is her stern that is swinging, pivoting on the bow. As the lights move apart the "range is opening." As they come closer together, the "range is closing." ***Be alert for sudden course changes, indicated by the lights changing position.*** Remember, large cargo vessels have a hard time maneuvering so allow plenty of room. If necessary, contact them on VHF Ch. 16 (156.800) Mhz).

Stephen B. Roman at Lock 7 on the Welland Canal, 26 July, 1995.

Roger LeLievre

PLIMSOLL MARKINGS

The Plimsoll Mark is a load line on the side of a ship's hull. It shows how much cargo the ship can carry safely under different conditions. The position of the marking depends on the type and size of the vessel. The name came from the load-line markings on British merchant ships owned by Samuel Plimsoll. It was through Plimsoll's efforts that an Act of Parliament to prevent overloading of vessels was passed. A ship "loaded down to her marks" carries capacity cargo - any more would lessen the chance of a safe voyage.

Load lines on American ships were established by the American Bureau of Shipping, provided by the Load Line Act of 1929, and apply to deep sea vessels of 150 tons or more.

The distance between the Plimsoll Mark and the deck is the ship's "freeboard." Special markings were established in 1935 for Great Lakes and Atlantic/Pacific coast voyages.

Plimsoll Mark - Great Lakes

The letters **AB** signify Amercan Bureau of Shipping
The letters **LR** signify Lloyd's Registry of Shipping
The letters **FW** signify load line in fresh water
The letters **SW** signify load line in salt water*
The letters **MS** signify midsummer
load (May 1- Sept. 15)
The letter **S** signifies summer load
line (April 26-30 and Sept. 16-30)
The letter **I** signifies intermediate
load line (April 1-15 and Oct. 1-31)
The letter **W** signifies winter load
line (Nov.1 to March 31)

The salt water marks are assigned only to vessels intending to load in salt water of the St. Lawrence River.

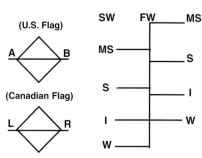

Some other markings you may see on foreign flag vessels:

The letters **LL** signify Lloyd's of London
The letter **T** signifies load line in tropical waters
The letters **TF** signify load line in tropical fresh water
The letters **WNA** apply to winter, North Atlantic load line

Algontario in winter lay-up, 1995-'96, at Windsor, ON.

Todd L. Davidson

CARGO RECORDS

Cargo	Vessel	Net Tonnage	Gross Tonnage	Year
Cement	**Alpena**	13,700	12,232	1994
Eastern Coal *(Seaway)*				
	J.W. McGiffin	31,028	27,509	1972
Eastern Coal *(Soo)*				
	Indiana Harbor	60,578	53,708	1994
Iron ore				
Lake Ontario	**Simcoe**	29,114	25,995	1972
Great Lakes	**Lewis Wilson Foy**	81,033	72,351	1986
Seaway	**Paterson**	31,922	28,502	1986
Soo	**Indiana Harbor**	72,117	64,391	1986
Limestone	**Oglebay Norton**	59,078	52,749	1992
Mixed Grain				
Oats	**Saguenay**	1,446,727	bushels	1964
Rye	**Senneville**	1,026,983	bushels	1975
Western Coal *(Lake Superior)*				
	Indiana Harbor	71,369	63,276	1993
Western Coal *(Soo)*				
	Columbia Star	70,706	62,688	1986

Rod Burdick

Indiana Harbor at the coal dock in Marquette.

GREAT LAKES ALBUM

Once the "racehorse of the Great Lakes," the speedy Cliffs Victory was sold overseas in 1985. A converted World War II Victory ship, she was the only laker to sport a cargo hold aft of the engine room.

Another fast vessel was the passenger steamer City of Erie. In a well-publicized, 1901 challenge, she raced the crack Detroit River liner Tashmoo from Cleveland to Toledo, and won.

Great Lakes passenger steamer North American at Charlevoix in years gone by.

Since vessels of the Minnesota-Atlantic Transit Co. were named Ten, Jack, King, Queen and Ace, the company was nicknamed 'The Poker Fleet.'

Arthur B. Homer, seen here from Detroit's Ambassador Bridge, was scrapped at Port Colborne in 1986.

Richard I. Weiss

Socanav tanker Le Saule No. 1 passes Marysville.

Panoramic view of the 1,000-footer Oglebay Norton at dusk near the Soo.

Roger LeLievre

Terry Sechen

Seaway Queen at Duluth.

John R. Emery unloads sand at Erie. *Roger LeLievre*

Jim Bearman

Richard Reiss makes room for loading spouts by swinging her boom off to one side.

MUSEUMS & HISTORIC VESSELS

A-Admission fee; **T**-Tours; **G**-Gift Shop

(Information subject to change; museum hours can vary. Phone ahead.)

VESSEL MUSEUMS

Willis B. Boyer - Owned by the city of Toledo, OH, this 1911-built steamer is located on the Maumee River at International Park.
419-936-3070 - A,T,G - *Year' 'round (call for winter hours) - Volunteers needed*

H.M.C.S. Haida - World War II-era, Canadian destroyer is credited with the destruction of 14 enemy ships.
416-314-9900 -A- Ontario Place, 955 Lakeshore Blvd., Toronto, ON.
May 21-Oct. 14

Alexander Henry - Operated by the Marine Museum of the Great Lakes at Kingston, this former Canadian Coast Guard icebreaker is open for tours and as a bed and breakfast.
613-542-2261 - A,T,G - 55 Ontario St., Kingston, ON. *May-Sept..*

Huron - The 97-foot lightship Huron guided mariners into lower Lake Huron leading to the St. Clair River for 36 years, until replaced by lighted bouys in 1970.
810-985-7101 - A,T - Pine Grove Park, Port Huron, MI. *Mid-May-Sept.*

William A. Irvin - Built in 1938, the 610-foot-long Irvin is the former flagship of the U.S. Steel fleet. She last sailed in 1972.
218-722-7876 - A,T,G - Duluth & Area Convention Center, 350 Harbor Dr., Duluth, MN. - *Late spring-fall*

Keewatin - The coal-burning passenger steamer Keewatin, which sailed the lakes for Canadian Pacific Railway from 1907 until her retirement in 1965, is now open to the public at Douglas, on Lake Michigan's south shore. Also on display: tug Reiss.
616-857-2464 or 616-857-2107 - A,T,G - *Memorial Day-Labor Day*

William G. Mather - Harbor Heritage Society operates the museum ship Mather, a former Cleveland-Cliffs iron ore carrier, at the E. Ninth Street pier in Cleveland. Displays and artifacts help tell the story of the Great Lakes shipping industry. **Adjacent to the Rock and Roll Hall of Fame.**
216-574-6262 - A,T,G - *May-Oct.*

Cont'd on Page 112

Meteor - Built in 1897 the Meteor, open for tours on Barker's Island in Superior, WI, is the last example of the "whaleback" design common on the lakes in the early 1900s. Also on display is the dipper dredge Col. D.D. Gaillard, built in 1916.

715-392-5742 or 715-392-1083. - A,T,G - Head of the Lakes Maritime Society, Superior WI. - *May-mid-Oct.*

Niagara - Commodore Oliver Hazard Perry's flagship, the U.S.S. Niagara, has been extensively rebuilt and opened to the public. From the Niagara's decks, Perry proclaimed "We have met the enemy and they are ours," during the War of 1812's Battle of Lake Erie.

814-452-2744 (phone ahead to make sure ship is in port). - A,T - Pennsylvania Historical & Museum Commission, Erie, PA.

Norgoma - Although this former Georgian Bay-area freight and passenger ferry is still undergoing renovation, she is open to the public at Roberta Bondar Park on the Sault Ste. Marie, ON waterfront.

705-256-7447 - A,T,G - St. Mary's River Marine Center - *Mid-April - Oct.*

Norisle - This former Georgian Bay-area passenger/freight carrier is open as a museum in Heritage Park, Manitowaning, ON.

705-859-3977 - A,T - *June 1-Labor Day*

Nash - This former U.S. Army Corps of Engineers tug, built in 1943, is the only known surviving Army vessel associated with D-Day.

At the H. Lee White Marine Museum, 1176 Niagara St., Oswego, NY.

U.S.S. Cobia - see Wisconsin Maritime Museum, Page 116
U.S.S. Cod - see Great Lakes Historical Society, Page 114
U.S.S. Croaker - see Naval and Serviceman's Park Museum, Page 116
U.S.S. Little Rock - see Naval and Serviceman's Park Museum, Page 116
U.S.S. Silversides - Restored World War II submarine, one of war's most highly-decorated, is open to the public at Muskegon, MI.

616-755-1230 - A,T - *April-Oct.*

U.S.S. The Sullivans - see Naval and Serviceman's Park Museum, Page 116

Valley Camp - Berthed at the foot of Johnstone Street in Sault Ste. Marie, MI, this 1917-built ore and coal carrier is now home of an extensive Great Lakes marine museum operated by Le Sault de Sainte Marie Historic Sites. Cargo holds house artifacts, ship models, photos and other memorabilia, as well as a tribute to the *Edmund Fitzgerald* that includes the ship's two lifeboats. Historic Sites also operates the nearby Tower of History, a 21-story observation tower that offers an excellent view of the Soo Locks and Soo Harbor.

906-632-3658 - A,T,G - *May 15-Oct.15*

HISTORIC HULLS *(NOT OPEN TO THE PUBLIC)*

Canadiana - At this writing, 1916-built passenger ship is in sadly deteriorated shape near Port Colborne, ON. Major refurbishing is needed before she can assume her role as a historic attraction in Buffalo, NY.

Clipper - 1905-built passenger steamer (ex. *Milwaukee Clipper, Juniata*) faces an uncertain future as a civic attraction at Hammond, IN.

City of Milwaukee - Former Lake Michigan rail and passenger ferry, built in 1931, awaits conversion to a musuem at Frankfort, MI.

Edna G - Lake County Historical Society in Two Harbors, MN. owns this 1896-vintage steam-powered tug, which served the area for more than eight decades. Refurbished in 1994.

Niagara - Retired Great Lakes sandsucker awaits conversion to a museum at Erie, PA.

Niagara at Erie.
Jim Thoreson

MAJOR MARINE MUSEUMS ASHORE

Antique Boat Museum, *750 Mary St., Clayton, NY.* Extensive collection of historic freshwater boats and engines. Annual boat show first weekend of August. **315-686-4104 - A,G** - *May 15-Oct. 15*

Bernier Maritime Museum, *55 rue des Pionniers Est., L'Islet-Sur-Mer, PQ..* Located in an 1877-built convent, the museum explores the history of navigation on the St. Lawrence River. Several vessels are displayed, including the icebreaker *Ernest Lapointe.* **418-247-5001 - A** - *Open year 'round*

Canal Park Marine Museum, *Duluth, MN.* Operating steam engine, full-size replicas of cabins as found on Great Lakes ships, and numerous hands-on exhibits. - **218-727-2497 - Operated by the U.S. Army Corps of Engineers,- Free** - *Open year 'round*

Collingwood Marine Museum, *Collingwood, ON.* More than 100 years of shipbuilding, illustrated with models, photos and videos. **705-445-4811 - A,G** - *Open year 'round.*

Door County Maritime Museum, *Sunset Park, Sturgeon, Bay, WI.* Located in the former offices of the Roen Steamship Co., exhibits portray the role shipbuilding has played in the Door Peninsula. Displays include artifacts from sunken ships, photos and charts. Refurbished pilothouse on display. **414-743-8139 - A (donations)** - *Memorial Day-mid-Oct.*

Dossin Great Lakes Museum, *100 The Strand Dr., Belle Isle, Detroit, MI.* Ship models, photographs, interpretive displays, the smoking room from the 1912 passenger steamer *City of Detroit III,* an anchor from the *Edmund Fitzgerald* and the working pilothouse from the steamer *William Clay Ford* are just a few of this museum's wide range of attractions. **313-267-6440 - A (donations),G -** *Open year 'round.*

Fathom Five National Marine Park, *Tobermory, ON.* Canada's first national underwater maritime park encompasses 19 of the area's 26 shipwrecks, two of which can be seen from a glass-bottom boat. **519-596-2233 - A -** *April-mid-Nov.*

Great Lakes Historical Society, *480 Main St., Vermilion, OH.* Extensive museum tells the story of the Great Lakes through ship models, paintings, exhibits and artifacts, including engines and other machinery. Pilothouse of retired laker *Canopus* and a replica of the Vermilion lighthouse are also on display. **216-967-3467 - A,G -** *museum open year 'round.* An affiliated operation is the *U.S.S. Cod,* a World War II submarine open to the public in Cleveland harbor. *May 1-Labor Day ... tour restrictions may apply -* call **216-566-8770** *for details.* **- A,T,G**

Great Lakes Marine & U.S. Coast Guard Memorial Museum, *1071-73 Walnut Blvd., Ashtabula, OH.* Housed in 1898-built former lighthouse keepers' residence, museum includes models, paintings, artifacts, photos, the world's only working scale model of a Hulett ore unloading machine and the pilothouse from the steamer *Thomas Walters.* **216-964-6847 - A (donations) - T,G -** *Memorial Day-Oct. 31*

Great Lakes Shipwreck Historical Museum, *Whitefish Point, MI.* Located next to the historic Whitefish Point lighthouse, the museum houses extensive lighthouse and shipwreck artifacts, a shipwreck video theater and an *Edmund Fitzgerald* display that includes the ship's bell. **906- 635-1742 -A,G -** *May 15-Oct. 15*

Marine Museum of Upper Canada, *Exhibition Place, Toronto, ON.* Exhibits detail the development of the shipping industry on the Great Lakes and St. Lawrence Seaway. The restored, 80-foot steam tug *Ned Hanlan,* built in 1932, is also open to visitors. **416-392-1765 - A,G -** *Museum open year 'round (tug seasonal only)*

Marquette Maritime Museum, *East Ridge and Lakeshore Dr., Marquette, MI.* Contained in an 1890s water works building, the museum has recreated the offices of the first commercial fishing and passenger freight companies. Displays also include charts, photos, models and maritime artifacts. **906-226-2006 - A -** *May 31-Sept. 30*

Michigan Maritime Museum, *off I-196 at Dyckman Ave (exit 20), South Haven, MI.* Exhibits dedicated to the U.S. Lifesaving Service and U.S. Coast Guard, and displays that tell the story of boats and their uses on the Great Lakes. **616-637-8078 - A,G -** *Open year 'round.*

Museum of Science and Industry, *57th Street and Lakeshore Dr., Chicago, ILL.* Among the museum's displays is the captured World War II German submarine *U-505,* built in Hamburg in 1941. **312-684-1414 - A,T -** *Open year 'round*

'Whaleback'-style oil tanker Meteor, open to the public at Superior, WI. See Page 112.

Richard I. Weiss

Naval and Serviceman's Park Museum, *foot of Main and Pearl streets,* *Buffalo, NY.* On display: the guided missile cruiser **U.S.S. Little Rock,** the WW2 destroyer **U.S.S. The Sullivans** and the WW2 submarine **U.S.S. Croaker.** Museum displays include models, armed service artifacts and aircraft. **716-847-1773 - A,T,G -** *April-Nov.*

Old Mariners' Church, *170 E. Jefferson Ave., Detroit, Mi.* Church was built in 1849 on Woodward Ave. originally, but was moved in 1955 to make way for a civic center. The blessing of the Great Lakes fleet and a memorial service for those who have died at sea takes place on the second Sunday of March. A memorial service is held for the crew of the **Edmund Fitzgerald** on the Sunday closest to Nov. 10. Normal services are held every Sunday at 11 a.m. The annual blessing of the fleet is held in March. **313-259-2206 - T (reservations required), A (donation)**

Owen Sound Marine-Rail Museum, *1165 First Ave., Owen Sound, ON.* Museum depicts the history of each industry through displays, photos. **519-371-3333. - A -**

Point Iroquois Light Station, *Point Iroquois, MI (20 mi. west of Sault Ste. Marie)* Museum in historic lighthouse reveals the stories of lightkeepers and their families. Climbers can get a breathtaking view from the top of the tower. Renovation undertaken in 1983 by the Bay Mills-Brimley Historical Research Society and the U.S. Forestry Service. **906-635-5311 -** *Memorial Day-Labor Day*

Port Colborne Historical and Marine Museum, *280 King St.,Port Colborne, ON.* Wheelhouse from the steam tug **Yvonne Dupre Jr.,** anchor from the propellor ship **Raleigh,** and a lifeboat from the steamer **Hochelaga** are among the musuem's displays. **905-834-7604 - Free -** *May-Dec.*

River of History Museum, *Old Federal Bldg., Portage Ave. at Bingham Ave., Sault Ste. Marie, MI.* Interpretive display explores 8,000 years of history of the St. Mary's River Valley, from glacial origins to Native American occupation, the French fur trade, British expansion and the U.S. creation of a state. **906-632-1999 - A,G -**

Sandpoint Lighthouse, *Escanaba, Mi.* Restored, 1867-vintage lighthouse. **906-786-3763 - A -** *June 1-Labor Day*

U.S. Army Corps of Engineers Museum, *Soo Locks Visitor Center, Sault Ste. Marie, MI.* Includes a working model of the Soo Locks, photos depicting their history, and a 25-minute film. Also, three outdoor observation decks adjacent to the MacArthur Lock provide an up-close view of ships locking through. **- Free -** *May-Nov.*

Welland Canal Visitor Center, *Thorold, ON.* Museum traces the history and development of the Welland Canal. The pilothouse of the package freighter **Fort Henry** *is also on* display. **905-685-3711 - G -** *Museum open year 'round. Observation deck open during the navigation season.*

Wisconsin Maritime Museum, *75 Maritime Dr., Manitowoc, WI.* Extensive displays on the history of shipbuilding. The exhibit also honors submariners and submarine-building in Manitowoc during World War 2. The submarine **U.S.S. Cobia,** built in 1943, is open for tours. **414-684-0218 - A,G,T -** *open year 'round*

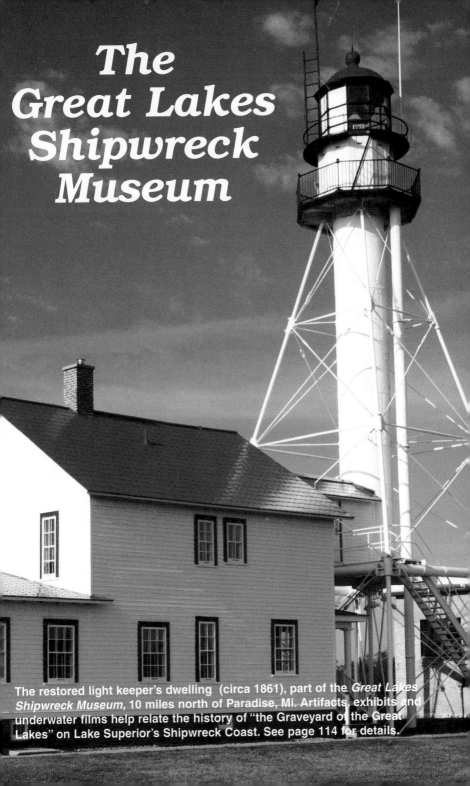

The Great Lakes Shipwreck Museum

The restored light keeper's dwelling (circa 1861), part of the *Great Lakes Shipwreck Museum*, 10 miles north of Paradise, Mi. Artifacts, exhibits and underwater films help relate the history of "the Graveyard of the Great Lakes" on Lake Superior's Shipwreck Coast. See page 114 for details.

Spotlight on ...
Canada Steamship Lines

Founded in 1845, Canada Steamship Lines has long been an innovator, not only on the Great Lakes and St. Lawrence Seaway shipping scene, but internationally as well.

Long-considered a pioneer in the development of self-unloading technology, CSL's first such vessel, the tiny **Collier** of 1924, began a trend towards independence from shoreside cargo handling equipment that is the standard today. CSL is also known for refining the art of package-freight handling, and holds a key place in history for its role in the planning and construction of the Seaway, opened in 1959. Once the waterway was completed, CSL again took the lead, quickly placing orders for maximum-sized vessels like the 730-foot **Murray Bay (i),** built in 1960.

In the 1980s, CSL looked towards saltwater for its next phase of growth, building **Atlantic Superior** in 1982 for combined lakes/ocean service. In 1990, **CSL Atlas** arrived for exclusive service on saltwater. In 1995 the company ordered three new vessels which will be used to explore markets in Southeast Asia, a sure sign more chapters are forthcoming in the history of this pioneering enterprise.

Early CSL self-unloader Coalhaven, built in 1928.

Colors of the Great Lakes and Seaway Smokestacks

Algoma Central Marine Navigation Sonamar
Sault Ste. Marie, ON

American Tug & Transit Co.
Bay City, MI

American Steamship Co.
Williamsville, NY

Andrie, Inc.
Muskegon, MI

Arnold Transit Co.
Mackinac Island, MI

Beaver Island Transit Co.
Charlevoix, MI

Bethlehem Steel Corp.
Chesterton, IN

Bignane Vessel Fueling Co.
Chicago, IL

Stacks, on ships as buildings, serve two purposes—to vent smoke and produce an air draft for the boilers. Early steamships had single-shell stacks, which got quite hot. The modern ship's stack, or funnel is really two stacks. The space between the lining (inner cylinder) and the casing (outer cylinder) provides an air jacket convenient for keeping the outer cool and also for ventilation.

The relatively cool casing of modern stacks can be permanently painted any color, from brilliant hues to complicated monograms and trademarks.

Many of today's vessels don't need a traditional smokestack, but because popular illusion leads one to think that a vessel without a stack has something wrong with it, most carry one for the sake of appearance.

B+B Dredging Corp.
Crystal River, FL

Canada Steamship Lines, Inc.
Montreal, PQ

Canadian Coast Guard
Ottawa, ON

Canadian Dredge & Dock Inc.
Don Mills, ON

Chicago Fire Department
Chicago, IL

Cleveland Fire Department
Cleveland, OH

Buffalo Fire Department
Buffalo, NY

Cleveland Tankers, Inc.
Cleveland, OH

Coastwise Trading Co.
East Chicago, IN

D
Dean Construction Co.
Belle River, ON

Diamond Jack River Tours
Detroit, MI

Duluth - Superior Excursions
Duluth, MN

Durocher Dock & Dredge, Inc.
Cheboygan, MI

Eastern Canada Towing Ltd.
Halifax, NS

Enerchem Transport, Inc.
Montreal, PQ

Erie Navigation Co.
Erie Sand & Gravel Co.
Erie, PA

Erie Sand Steamship Co.
Erie, PA

Essroc Canada, Inc.
Toronto, ON

Esso Petroleum Canada Div.
Imperial Oil Ltd.
Dartmouth, NS

Fednav International Ltd.
Montreal, PQ

Fraser Shipyards, Inc.
Superior, WI

Gaelic Tug Boat Co.
Grosse Ile, MI

Goodtime Transit Boats, Inc.
Cleveland, OH

Great Lakes Towing Co.
Cleveland, OH

Great Lakes Dredge & Dock Co.
Oak Brook, IL

Great Lakes Maritime Academy
Northwestern Michigan College
Traverse City, MI

Hannah Marine Corp.
Lemont, IL

Inland Lakes Management, Inc.
Alpena, MI

Lake Michigan Carferry Service, Inc.
Ludington, MI

Madeline Island Ferry Line, Inc.
LaPoint, WI

Miller Boat Line, Inc.
Put - In - Bay, OH

Pelee Island Transportation Services
Pelee Island, ON

Sandusky Boat Line
Sandusky, OH

LaFarge Canada, Inc.
Canada Steamship Lines - Mgr.
Montreal, PQ

MacDonald Marine Ltd.
Goderich, ON

Merce Transportation Co.
Sylvania, OH

N.M. Paterson & Sons Ltd.
Thunder Bay, ON

Roen Salvage Co.
Sturgeon Bay, WI

Kinsman Lines, Inc.
Cleveland, OH

Luedtke Engineering Co.
Frankfort, MI

Medusa Cement Co.
Division of Medusa Corp.
Cleveland, OH

P & H Shipping
Div. of Parrish & Heimbecker Ltd.
Mississauga, ON

Rideau St. Lawrence
Cruise Ships, Inc.
Kingston, ON

King Construction Co.
Holland, MI

Lower Lakes Towing
Port Dover, ON

McKeil Marine Ltd.
Hamilton, ON

Ontario Northland
Transportation Commission
Owen Sound, ON

Quebec Tugs Ltd.
Quebec, PQ

Kent Line Ltd
Saint John, NB

Lock Tours Canada
Sault Ste. Marie, ON

McAllister Towing & Salvage, Inc.
Montreal, PQ

Ontario Ministry of
Transportation & Communication
Kingston, ON

OMT Navigation, Inc.
Montreal, PQ

Kellstone, Inc.
Cleveland, OH

Litton Great Lakes Corp.
USS Great Lakes Fleet - Mgr.
Erie, PA

Marine Fueling Co.
St. Paul, MN

Oglebay Norton Co.
Cleveland, OH

J. W. Purvis Marine Ltd.
Sault Ste. Marie, ON

The Interlake Steamship Co.
Lakes Shipping Co.
Cleveland, OH

Lee Marine, Ltd.
Port Lambton, ON

Malcom Marine
St. Clair, MI

Neuman Boat Line, Inc.
Sandusky, OH

Provmar Fuels, Inc.
Div. of ULS Corporation
Toronto, ON

Inland Steel Co.
East Chicago, IN

Lake Michigan Contractors, Inc.
Holland, MI

Maid of the Mist Steamboat Co., Ltd.
Niagara Falls, ON

Muskoka Lakes Navigation &
Hotel Co
Gravenhurst, ON

Pioneer Shipping Ltd
Canada Steamship Lines - Man.
Winnipeg, MB

MUSEUM SHIPS

St. Mary's Cement Co.
Toronto, ON

St. Lawrence Seaway
Development Corp.
Massena, NY

St. Lawrence Seaway Authority
Cornwall, ON

Soo Locks Boat Tours
Sault Ste. Marie, MI

Socanav, Inc.
Montreal, PQ

Museum Ships
Willis B. Boyer (Toledo)
William G. Mather (Cleveland)

Museum Ships
Norgoma (Sault Ste. Marie)
Norisle (Manitowanic)

Museum Ship
USCGC Lightship 103
"Huron"
Port Huron, MI

Museum Ship
Valley Camp
Sault Ste. Marie, MI

Museum Ship
USCOE Nash
Otswego, NY

Museum Ship
Meteor
Superior, WI

Museum Ship
Keewatin
Douglas, MI

Museum Ship
William A. Irvin
Duluth, MN

Museum Ships
USS Little Rock
USS The Sullivans
Buffalo, NY

Museum Ship
Clipper
Hammond, IN

Museum Ship
CGCG Alexander Henry
Kingston, ON

Museum Ship
HMCS Haida
Toronto, ON

Shepler's Mackinac
Island Ferry Services
Mackinaw City, MI

ULS Corporation
Jackes Shipping, Inc.
ULS Marbulk, Inc.
Toronto, ON

United States
Environmental Protection Agency
Bay City, MI

Upper Lakes Towing Company, Inc.
Escanaba, MI

Shell Canada Products Ltd.
Montreal, PQ

Transport Desgagnes, Inc.
Quebec, PQ

United States Coast Guard
9th Coast Guard District
Cleveland, OH

University of Michigan
Center for Great Lakes
& Aquatic Sciences
Ann Arbor, MI

Selvick Marine Towing Corp.
Sturgeon Bay, WI

Star Line Fleet
St. Ignace, MI

United States Army-
Great Lakes - Corps of Engineers
Detroit, MI

USS Great Lakes Fleet, Inc.
Duluth, MN

Pilothouse of steamer William Clay Ford
is on display at Dossin Great Lakes
Museum in Detroit.

House Flags of Major Great Lakes & Seaway Shipping Companies

Algoma Central Marine

American Steamship Co.

Atlantic Towing Ltd. Kent Line Ltd.

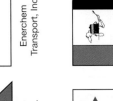

Bethlehem Steel Corp.

Canada Steamship Lines, Inc.

Cleveland Tankers, Inc.

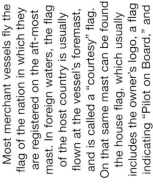

Enerchem Transport, Inc.

Erie Navigation Co.; Erie Sand & Gravel

Gaelic Tug Boat Co.

Great Lakes Towing Co.

Imperial Oil Ltd. Esso Petroleum Canada Div.

Inland Lakes Management, Inc.

Inland Steel Co.

Interlake Steamship Co. Lakes Shipping Co.

Kinsman Lines, Inc.

Oglebay Norton Co.

P. & H. Shipping

N.M. Paterson & Sons Ltd.

Seaway Bulk Carriers

Seaway Self Unloaders

Socanav, Inc. QMT Navigation, Inc.

Transport Desgagnes, Inc.

ULS Corporation

USS Great Lakes Fleet, Inc.

Most merchant vessels fly the flag of the nation in which they are registered on the aft-most mast. In foreign waters, the flag of the host country is usually flown at the vessel's foremast, and is called a "courtesy" flag. On that same mast can be found the house flag, which usually includes the owner's logo, a flag indicating "Pilot on Board," and the captain's personal flag reflecting his membership in the International Shipmaster's Association.

Flags of all Nations in the Marine Trade

United States

Afghanistan	Albania	Algeria	Angola	Antigua & Barbuda	Belize	Benin	Bermuda
Argentina	Armenia	Australia	Austria	Azerbaijan	Cameroon	Cape Verde	Chile
Bahamas	Bahrain	Bangladesh	Barbados	Belgium	Croatia	Cuba	Cyprus
Bosnia & Herzegovnia	Brazil	Brunei	Bulgaria	Cambodia	Egypt	El Salvador	Equatorial Guinea
China	Colombia	Congo	Costa Rica	Cote D'Ivoire	France	French Polynesia	Gabon
Czech Republic	Denmark	Djibouti	Dominican Republic	Ecuador			
Eritrea	Estonia	Ethiopia	Fiji	Finland			

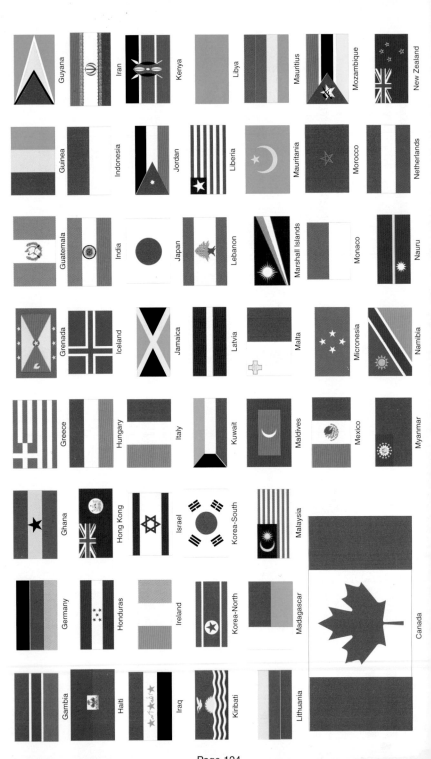

Guyana
Iran
Kenya
Libya
Mauritius
Mozambique
New Zealand

Guinea
Indonesia
Jordan
Liberia
Mauritania
Morocco
Netherlands

Guatemala
India
Japan
Lebanon
Marshall Islands
Monaco
Nauru

Grenada
Iceland
Jamaica
Latvia
Malta
Micronesia
Namibia

Greece
Hungary
Italy
Kuwait
Maldives
Mexico
Myanmar

Ghana
Hong Kong
Israel
Korea-South
Malaysia

Germany
Honduras
Ireland
Korea-North
Madagascar
Canada

Gambia
Haiti
Iraq
Kiribati
Lithuania

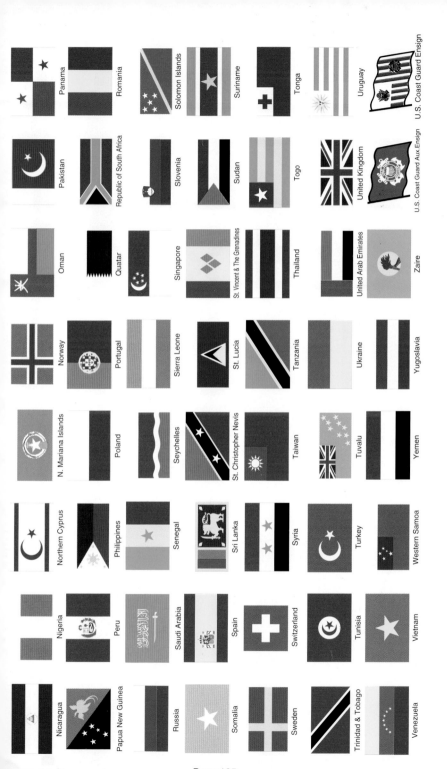

Panama
Romania
Solomon Islands
Suriname
Tonga
Uruguay
U.S. Coast Guard Ensign

Pakistan
Republic of South Africa
Slovenia
Sudan
Togo
United Kingdom
U.S. Coast Guard Aux Ensign

Oman
Qatar
Singapore
St. Vincent & The Grenadines
Thailand
United Arab Emirates
Zaire

Norway
Portugal
Sierra Leone
St. Lucia
Tanzania
Ukraine
Yugoslavia

N. Mariana Islands
Poland
Seychelles
St. Christopher Nevis
Taiwan
Tuvalu
Yemen

Northern Cyprus
Philippines
Senegal
Sri Lanka
Syria
Turkey
Western Samoa

Nigeria
Peru
Saudi Arabia
Spain
Switzerland
Tunisia
Vietnam

Nicaragua
Papua New Guinea
Russia
Somalia
Sweden
Trinidad & Tobago
Venezuela

Page 125

International Code Flags and Pennants

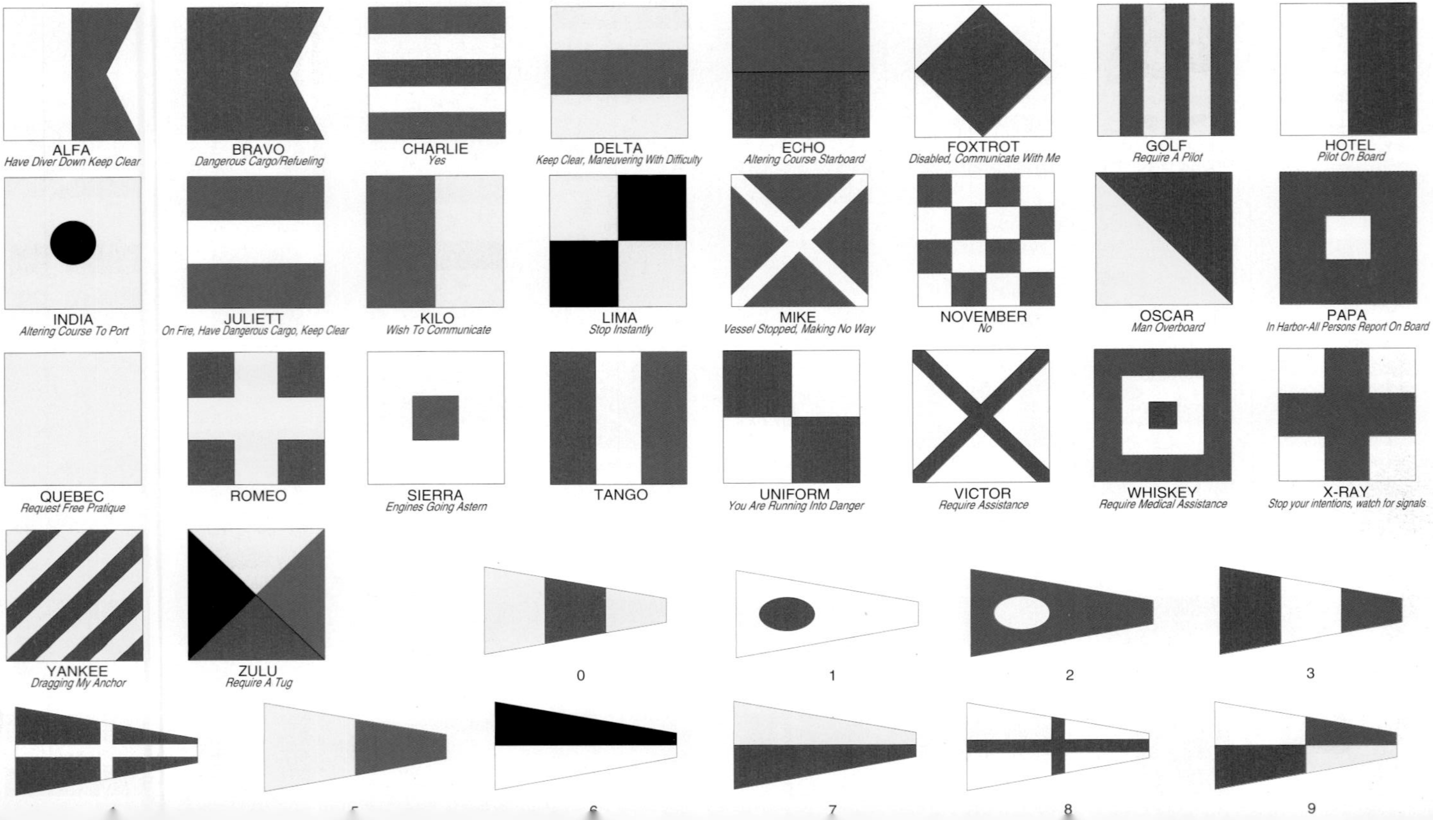

ALFA — Have Diver Down Keep Clear

BRAVO — Dangerous Cargo/Refueling

CHARLIE — Yes

DELTA — Keep Clear, Maneuvering With Difficulty

ECHO — Altering Course Starboard

FOXTROT — Disabled, Communicate With Me

GOLF — Require A Pilot

HOTEL — Pilot On Board

INDIA — Altering Course To Port

JULIETT — On Fire, Have Dangerous Cargo, Keep Clear

KILO — Wish To Communicate

LIMA — Stop Instantly

MIKE — Vessel Stopped, Making No Way

NOVEMBER — No

OSCAR — Man Overboard

PAPA — In Harbor-All Persons Report On Board

QUEBEC — Request Free Pratique

ROMEO

SIERRA — Engines Going Astern

TANGO

UNIFORM — You Are Running Into Danger

VICTOR — Require Assistance

WHISKEY — Require Medical Assistance

X-RAY — Stop your intentions, watch for signals

YANKEE — Dragging My Anchor

ZULU — Require A Tug

Numeral Pennants: 0 1 2 3 ... 9

Repeater Pennants: 6 7 8 9

Also from MARINE PUBLISHING CO., INC.

STACK & FLAG CHART

20" x 30" full-color chart shows the stack colors and house flags of Great Lakes and Seaway fleets, flags of nations in the marine trade, code and signal flags and more. $14.95

(Laminated, add $3)

SHIPWRECK CHART

100 major Great Lakes & Seaway disasters, detailed on a 20" x 30," three-color wall chart, printed on parchment-style paper; with photographs. Perfect for cottage or den. $14.95 (Laminated, add $3)

PHOTOS

Photographs of most Great Lakes vessels currently in service are available for purchase. Price depends on size - please write for price list. Photos of older ships may also be on file - please write for availability.

'KNOW YOUR SHIPS' - Back Issues

'Know Your Ships' 1995 .... $12.95
Issues of 'Know Your Ships' for '94, '93, '92, '91, '90, '89, '88, '87, '86, '85, '84, '83, '82, '81, '79, '78, '77, '76 and '70 are still available. .... $6.50 ea.

VIDEOS

GREAT LAKES SHIPS IN ACTION (VHS only)
Excellent footage of nearly 100 vessels (several of which are no longer in service), from tugs to 1,000- footers, set to relaxing classical music (no narration). Approx. 50 minutes long. **$39.95**

Call or write our two locations ...

P. O. Box 68
Sault Ste. Marie, MI 49783
(906) 632-8417

317 S. Division St., Ste 8
Ann Arbor, MI 48104
(313) 668-4734 (phone & FAX)
E-mail: rlkysbook@aol.com

Michigan orders, add 6% sales tax
Please include 10% shipping
~ All orders in U.S. funds ~

VISA / MASTERCARD ACCEPTED

Retail discounts available

Deck view of cement carrier J.W. Iglehart, looking aft from atop wheelhouse.